I·N·S·I·D·E
INSOMNIA

I·N·S·I·D·E
INSOMNIA

Bernard Dryer, M.D.,
& Ellen S. Kaplan

VILLARD BOOKS ▼ NEW YORK 1986

Library of Congress Cataloging in Publication Data

Dryer, Bernard V. (Bernard Victor)
Inside insomnia.

Includes index.
1. Insomnia.   2. Sleep disorders.   3. Sleep
disorders—Treatment.   I. Kaplan, Ellen S.   II. Title.
RC548.D79   1986   616.8′49   86-40100
ISBN 0-394-74619-8

Grateful acknowledgment is made to the following for permission to reprint previously published material:

Journal of the American Medical Association: excerpts from "Chronic Insomnia Provokes More Prescriptions than Diagnoses," by Quentin Regestein. Copyright 1977 by the American Medical Association. (April 11, 1977, Volume 237, No. 15, pg. 1569.)

Lexington Books: excerpts from *Society and Medication: Conflicting Signals for Prescribers and Patients,* edited by John P. Morgan and Doreen V. Kagan. (Lexington Mass: Lexington Books, D.C. Heath and Company, Copyright 1983, D.C. Heath and Company.)

The New York Times: excerpt from "Industrial Time Clock," by Nancy Perry, November 28, 1982. Copyright © 1982 by The New York Times Company. Reprinted by permission of *The New York Times.*

Text design by Dana Kasarsky Design

9 8 7 6 5 4 3 2

Manufactured in the United States of America

First Edition

For Bob, Evelyn, Daniel,
and
Joshua

O, I have passed a miserable night . . .

William Shakespeare, *Richard III*

CONTENTS

p·a·r·t · t·w·o
A READER'S GUIDE

"Sleep!"

Drawing by Wm. Steig; © 1953, 1981 The New Yorker Magazine, Inc.

A DOCTOR'S LETTER
TO THE READER

INSOMNIA IS THE MOST COMMON
MEDICAL COMPLAINT

Insomnia is the merry-go-round on which you—and millions of others—may find yourself taking a reluctant ride. Include your family and friends—all those who are close to you. They, too, will be affected by your sleeplessness.

Over and over again I've been impressed with how many of us have passed miserable nights struggling for some gentle slumber. How many of us know the familiar drumbeat of difficulties—the use and misuse of sleeping pills, jet lag, night/day work shifts, persistently heavy snoring, the obligatory nightly nightcap, sleep-related heartburn? Indeed, physicians in a national survey estimated that nearly one-fifth of their patients complain about insomnia.

A third of the United States' population is reported to have insomnia, with literally millions of sleeping pills taken nightly, tens of millions of such prescriptions written yearly, and even

more people buying nonprescription over-the-counter drugs for sleep.

To these numbers, add the legions of people who nightly try to drink themselves to sleep.

As I look back over the past twenty years or so, I'm struck by three observations:

- First, we doctors didn't know how little we knew about sleep/wake disorders, such as insomnia.
- Second, we felt we could treat the problem of troubled sleep with little more than a few pills and some reassurance.
- Third, words mean so many different things to different people. Five hours sleep nightly may be adequate for some, and grossly deficient for others, who call five-hours sleep per night insomnia. If you have had difficulty sleeping—going to sleep and staying asleep—your experience may fit this definition of insomnia: a repeated pattern of inability to sleep and wake in a balanced pattern, a pattern that previously had provided you with a feeling of satisfactory rest and capable activity. Frequently feeling unrefreshed in the morning is a pretty good way of identifying insomnia, although medical textbooks use additional descriptive terms, such as transient insomnia (over two-to-three weeks) or chronic insomnia (over months or years), or drug-dependency insomnia (caused by the misuse of drugs).

As the folk song goes, the times they are a-changin'. The day of the routinely prescribed sleeping pill seems to be on its way out. Because scientific research has replaced folklore, there is an optimistic shift in the treatment of insomnia. The National Institutes of Health gave recognition to this shift in a Consensus Conference that included primary care physicians, psychiatrists, biomedical researchers, and pharmacologists. The result was a nationally accepted, up-to-date, systematic

A DOCTOR'S LETTER TO THE READER

blueprint to clinical treatment. Among the ideas that came out of this across-the-board meeting are several that deserve special emphasis:

The Medical History

Making a careful health history the first step in the treatment of your insomnia can uncover specific conditions that may underlie your sleeplessness. Such a history would include answers to questions such as: Does your job put you under continuous pressure? Are you taking medications? Do you exercise? What do you drink? Eat? Do you use alcohol? Such questions sound very simple, but when added together they may present a revealing clinical picture. The range is as wide as human biology itself, cutting across all fields of medicine. The point is not the broad scope of the questions but the fact that they're being asked.

Sleep Medication Guidelines

Until recently, choosing a sleep medication was frequently a chancy enterprise. Many drugs were advertised, but there were few objective guidelines about which were effective. Doctors needed updated, universally endorsed evaluations of some vital questions, such as:

- Is this sleep medication safe and effective? for long-term treatment, or just for a few days? or at all?
- Will this sleep medication leave the patient with a morning-after chemical hangover?
- Which possible side effects are likely to occur?
- What is the likelihood of drug dependency and addiction?
- What precautions should be observed for the frail elderly?

A DOCTOR'S LETTER TO THE READER

Extensive scientific research in recent years has exposed the hazards and complicated body chemistry of sleep medications—both prescription and over-the-counter. Across the country, as well as the world, patients should benefit from the principles and information developed by the Consensus Conference—not only about when and how to choose among these medications but, most important, whether sleep medication is indicated for you at all.

Nondrug Treatment

The first line of therapy may very well be promising approaches that do not depend on sleep medication. These choices, including exercise, dietary changes, relaxation methods, and counseling, are now becoming commonplace.

Recent Developments

This book is a bridge between the latest findings of a young and growing field of medicine—sleep science—and you. Your facts, your information are the stepping stones to success in overcoming the affliction of insomnia. Despite the saying that a little bit of knowledge can be dangerous, it is my contention that every little bit can help you in this effort. And today, we're out in front.

There have been astounding and fascinating forays on the frontiers of sleep. Where there were islands of scientific inquiry twenty years ago, there is now a mapped continent of knowledge. These include:

- Codified classifications of sleep disorders for more precise diagnosis and treatment.
- New pharmacological understanding about how sleep medications work in your body and how multiple medications can backfire.

A DOCTOR'S LETTER TO THE READER

- New population profiles—who is taking psychoactive drugs (a group of drugs that includes your sleeping pills), at what age, and for what reasons.
- National associations for sleep-wake disorders, including sleep clinics worldwide.
- About one thousand articles published yearly on sleep, touching every aspect of science and medicine—psychiatry, internal medicine, neurology, pediatrics, pharmacology.
- New understanding about the role of stress in insomnia.

Today, as if we were astronauts discovering our inner space, we have observed, measured, recorded, theorized, tested—the whole spectrum of careful research that turns clinical theory into practical treatment and even cures. We have learned enough to be confident that once an accurate diagnosis is made, effective treatment is possible.

In the pages that follow, research breakthroughs and the evolving developments in sleep science are translated into easy-to-understand and workable ideas that can help you. Informed answers to your questions are critical to the success of your effort to overcome insomnia; they may even be lifesaving.

This practical guidebook to overcoming sleeplessness—both temporary and longlasting—can improve your ability to make informed judgments about your sleep needs and to sort out and select from a range of treatment, including:

- The changes—some quite effortless—frequently required for restful sleep.
- An examination of individual life styles, patterns of behavior, medication misuse and abuse, and pain and illness that often interfere with restorative sleep.
- The promising and encouraging possibility of lasting and safe relief from insomnia through nondrug therapies.

A DOCTOR'S LETTER TO THE READER

Use *Inside Insomnia* flexibly—in a traditional stem-to-stern reading, or by jumping to a chapter of special interest to you. The Reader's Guide, including useful resource lists and glossary, is Part II of this handbook, but may very well be your beginning to overcoming the distress, and often anguish, of sleeplessness. The point—the starting point—is to touch your life at its insomnia connections . . . and help you to break them.

A single idea from these pages that works for you can make a difference. If the far-reaching frustrations of insomnia, confusion and potential dangers of sleep medications, and the disruptions in your life are your experience, take heart. Help is on the way.

Bernard Dryer, M.D.

·p·a·r·t · o·n·e·

INSOMNIA
CONNECTIONS

·1·

SLEEPING, WAKING, DREAMING: THE ETERNAL TRIANGLE

There are few areas of human behavior so intimately related to your sense of well-being as sleep. If you consider that you spend about one-third of your life sleeping, and that those hours have a profound influence on your awake self, you may find it worthwhile to take a few minutes to scan your sleep data base for some of the basic ABC facts and ideas of the latest sleep knowledge. The accuracy of your information can often make the difference in your overcoming a sleep problem.

SOME PRESENT-DAY SLEEP MYTHS

In spite of extensive information available today on the nature of sleep, the effects of sleep medications and how they work in the body, and the broad media attention the subject of sleep receives, some long-held notions persist and even now defy new research to the contrary. Let's look at a few of these myths.

Sleep as Nothingness

For thousands of years, sleep was understood as nothingness, as a kind of total oblivion into which you fell each night, there to be restored for the next day. It seemed a passive experience: Your body hardly moved, your eyes were closed, your meaningful speech stopped, your mind was a blank. The unmoving body of the sleeper appeared as a kind of death in life. Indeed, from antiquity on, the vocabulary of death borrowed the vocabulary of sleep:

> Duncan is in his grave;
> After life's fitful fever, he sleeps well.

> William Shakespeare, *Macbeth,* Act III, Scene II

Sleep as Dreaming

Dreaming was a "something" in the nothingness of sleep and was believed to be the only thing happening in the brain during the hours of slumber. The mystery of dreaming monopolized interest as the most important part of sleep. Because of its drama, dreaming diverted attention from that part of sleep that appeared passive.

Old patterns of thought are hard to give up. Consider, for example, the following old wives' tales:

- You need at least seven to eight hours of sleep each night.
- Alcohol helps you fall asleep.
- Insomnia is always a sign that you're anxious.
- You can restore normal sleep with sleep medication.
- Heavy snoring means you're sleeping soundly.
- Jet lag can be prevented by extra sleep before traveling.
- Sex is a sure-fire sleep aid.

These are myths. They can profoundly affect your daily life and are all wrong. They are not trivial assumptions. They are serious misinformation. Ignorance can be literally life-threatening, especially if you have airway breathing problems and seek relief from a sleep disturbance through drugs.

SLEEP AND WAKEFULNESS

The nature of sleep has traditionally been a magnet of speculation. Is sleep a background state of existence to which we periodically revert, or the opposite, a disturber of the "natural" waking state? To some, the question of why we sleep is less intriguing than why we stay awake. These issues may sound philosophical, but in fact they have spurred research advances.

Recall that about one-third of our lives is spent in slumber. This rather far-reaching observation overlooks the despair of so many seeking that elusive one-third and surprisingly disregards that two-thirds of our lives is spent awake. Sleeping and waking are, in fact, inextricably woven together. Consider, for example, these findings:

- The latest discoveries from sleep science laboratories, using sensitive electronic equipment, have confirmed that the brain is active throughout the sleeping hours—not only just when you're awake.
- Some experts theorize that you are never completely asleep, only less awake, and that sleep is a kind of very subdued level of wakefulness. It's as if the volume control knob on your radio or television set were always set at louder or softer but never set at off.
- Wakefulness and sleep are viewed on a sliding scale of lessened to greater awareness.

- During the phases of sleep in which dreaming occurs, the electrical activity of the brain resembles wakefulness more than it does the other sleep phases.

It appears, in short, that the border between sleep and wakefulness may not be a border at all.

Researchers today consider sleep and wakefulness as two separate states of consciousness. A third state, called REM sleep, added to the other two, represents the latest understanding of the three fundamental states of existence. REM, or rapid eye movement under closed eyelids during sleep, is that part of sleep during which most dreaming occurs. Rather than accept sleep only as an absence of wakefulness, or REM sleep as only one part of sleep, scientists believe there are three interacting systems: sleeping, waking, and REM sleep.

THE STAIRCASE OF SLEEP

Sleep research, like space physics, is a child of twentieth-century technology. Once the brain was understood as a kind of miniature electric generator, sophisticated electronic equipment could be used to measure the differing electric potentials of its unceasing activity. At a glance—either on a graph-paper readout or on a computer monitor—astonishing differences between one network of nerve impulses and another could be seen.

For example, the wavy-line squiggles of brain activity during early sleep typically look like this:

non-REM

Ninety minutes later, however, they look like this:

REM

These characteristic electronic signatures may now pinpoint previously baffling sleep disorders. The significance of
this "decoding" of an electrical message means that thousands
of people can now get treatment on target at a savings in time,
cost, and everyday living.

The new sleep science has spawned a new vocabulary. Even
in as nontechnical a source as your newspaper, you might read
such terms as REM, non-REM, brain potentials, alpha waves,
sleep disorders, and polysomnographs. If you feel this scientific language needs translation, you have lots of company. But
if you have a serious sleep problem, it helps to remember that
sleep is not an electronic tracing on a measuring device, just
as tracks in the snow are not the skier. Sleep is a behavioral
state, a state of consciousness, and was so long before there
was high-tech equipment to discover its nature and measure
it. Indeed, while certain kinds of electronic tracings are associated with different levels of sleep, these same tracings may
also be noted when the "sleeper" is responding to drugs but
is awake or under anesthesia.

If we recognize that newly coined scientific terminology
can represent progress, we can appreciate its clinical significance. New terms are of more than academic interest; they
can be vital:

- The clinical importance of a growing ability to describe
  sleep is reflected in strengthened skills to define more precisely sleep disorders, make accurate diagnoses, prescribe
  appropriate treatments, and alleviate the sleep problem.
- A mighty host of health insurance, medical records, statistical analyses, computer transmission, disability benefits,

and legal aspects pivots on accurate language. Because this is an infant science, some of the language is still being minted and refined.

Several professional groups, such as the Association of Sleep Disorder Centers, have been working on a classification system. The American Medical Association has published *CPT* (*Current Procedural Terminology*), a volume whose goal is to "provide a uniform terminology" to effectively establish "nationwide communication among physicians, patients, and third parties."

The critical point is that sleep has been quantified and observations have been not only recorded but—more important—interpreted. The good news for the troubled sleeper is that success of treatment is linked to these observations and interpretations.

The basic findings are these: The outstanding observation is that there are two kinds, or states, of sleep. These differ from each other both physiologically and behaviorally. One kind is characterized by rapid eye movements beneath the closed lids. This part of sleep has been called "active" sleep, or REM sleep. Despite the fact that the sleeper is lying immobile with a diminished awareness of the environment, much of the body behaves as if it were awake:

- Peaks of biochemical, physiological, and psychological activity occur.
- There are variations in heartbeat, breathing, and blood pressure.
- The normal male has an erection and the normal female, vaginal excitation.
- Microscopic muscles within the ear contract as if the sleeper were listening intently.
- The eyeballs beneath the sleeper's closed lids seem to scan a moving image.

In contrast, if the sleeper has no rapid eye movements, is breathing slowly and regularly, with little or no muscle movement and with blood pressure lowered and regular, then he or she is in the non-REM state, or "quiet" sleep. Quiet sleep can be compared to a descent down a flight of stairs in which several "landings" have been defined as stages 1, 2, 3, and 4. The relaxed, drowsy sleeper begins the descent down the staircase by gradually succumbing to diminishing awareness. As the sleeper drifts into deeper sleep—progressing through stages 2, 3, and 4—the brain waves change, reflecting changing brain activity, as the sleeper goes "deeper." Quiet sleep and active sleep cycle rhythmically throughout the night, with quiet sleep normally preceding active sleep.

Today the classifications and descriptions of sleep patterns that have evolved are practical medical yardsticks. Disorders related to disturbed sleep patterns, even problems once considered uncommon or unimportant—such as the dislocation of work shift changes, the possible implications of heavy snoring, excessive daytime sleepiness, or chronic insomnia—can be more quickly recognized and treated.

Consider these advances:

• Long years of frustrating hit-and-miss treatment were frequently the norm for those so-called lazy people who repeatedly "catnapped" during the day and were lethargic even when awake. Such a person might suddenly fall asleep while laughing at a joke or even while driving a car. Major advances in understanding the processes and patterns of sleep—particularly REM sleep with which such people typically begin their sleeping—have defined this type of chronic drowsiness as narcolepsy, a surprisingly not-so-rare sleep disorder. On the other hand, a careful sleep history may in fact disclose that such a person's overwhelming lethargy is symptomatic of one of an assembly of illnesses of disordered consciousness, and might possibly indicate a metabolic, endocrine, neurologic, or psychiatric condition. Expert help may be needed—this is not a do-it-yourself effort.

- A child with persistent night terrors might, until recently, be viewed simply as having had many bad dreams. Today's medicine can go far beyond such a folkloric and incorrect description and differentiate among night terrors, nightmares, epilepsy, and sleepwalking. With an accurate diagnosis, effective treatment can begin immediately.

- Many considerations underlie the problem of male impotence, a condition that may be caused by psychological factors, anatomic reasons, drug reactions, or medical illness. When an accurate diagnosis remains out of reach of traditional methods, specialized techniques using sleep laboratory measurements may provide an answer.

SLEEP: HOW MANY HOURS ARE ENOUGH?

One of the practical applications of sleep research into the levels of sleep—particularly into the vague boundaries between sleep and wakefulness—is recognizing the occurrence of low-grade daytime sleepiness—a sleepiness that may subtly haunt your daytime hours.

You may rationalize that a daily on-and-off fatigue is an ordinary part of the human condition, like the universal common cold, and comes with the territory.

After all, healthy young students, shift workers, travelers, moonlighters, vacationers, entire families, millions of people find it commonplace to ignore the familiar but hardly noticeable feeling of low-grade sleepiness. We simply accept, or do not pay attention to, how the intense pace of the contemporary world—or how we cope with the sometimes too many

SLEEPING, WAKING, DREAMING

demands of our lives—is distorting what should be a comfortable balance between our sleeping and waking hours.

If you feel you are doing less than your best because of chronic daytime tiredness, commonsense, that reliable compass, may point at the simple observation that you are not getting enough sleep. Indeed, a question often asked of doctors about sleep is "How many hours are normal?"

It may be hard to accept the idea—for example, if you are trying to establish work-safety rules for on-the-job hours—but there are no fixed norms, only statistically average ranges. Seven to eight hours may appear to be an accepted average for an adult. But there are people who sleep two hours nightly and those who sleep nine or even twelve hours regularly, without complaint.

You won't find insurance-type tables for your age, weight, and height to tell you the exact number of hours you need. There are no hard-and-fast rules. No one seems to know yet exactly why we sleep—there may be many reasons—and therefore, trying to live up to a requirement of a specific number of hours is not only unscientific, it won't work.

If you're still concerned, however, about the number of hours of sleep you need and aren't getting, you'll be encouraged to learn that whatever number of hours works for you is the right amount. If those hours leave you feeling energetic and alert the next morning, this is good news: You've met your sleep needs. The flexibility in this principle makes good common sense and is reassuring.

• The belief that sleep should occur almost instantaneously, continue for eight hours, and be uninterrupted throughout the night runs counter to these facts:

Falling asleep may ordinarily take twenty to thirty minutes.

You are likely to have brief awakenings for two to three seconds during the course of the night. These normal miniarousals vary in number from five to ten in a young adult, to 150 in an elderly person.

- You may have unreasonable expectations about the amount of sleep you need. A "short sleeper"—someone sleeping fewer than seven hours nightly without any problem with daytime tiredness—may be mistakenly convinced that such brief sleep duration isn't normal. Trying to sleep longer, to force an unwilling sleep, may lead to hours of tossing and turning. Just because you sleep fewer than the supposed average of seven or eight hours doesn't mean that you have insomnia. If you are measuring yourself against a theoretical sleep norm and believe that you aren't getting the number of hours you think you need, you may fall into the trap of expecting to perform poorly the next day . . . and then doing just that.

- Evidence of adequate or inadequate nighttime sleep is how well you function the next day, not the number of hours you may have slept. The quality of your sleep, the sense of being rested and energetic, is as important as the quantity of your sleep. If you are short-tempered, increasingly tired, if you're slowed down in your body movements with an underpar reaction time and attention gaps, you may need either more sleep or a different sleep-and-wakefulness pattern. A midday nap might give you a lift, although a pattern of long siestas could subtract hours from your "regular" nighttime sleep.

- Not only will you differ considerably from someone else in the amount of sleep you need, but the individual patterns of your sleep and wakefulness will themselves vary over your lifetime.

It seems natural to attribute low-grade daytime sleepiness to inadequate nighttime sleep. But the spectrum of organic problems masquerading as sleepiness—and incidentally contributing to sleepless hours at night—is a medical challenge for any professional.

The manifold faces of fatigue—a genuine buzzword in the lexicon of clinical symptoms—underline the importance of not overlooking pathological conditions, such as depression, anemia, low blood pressure, sleep apnea, or narcolepsy. A doctor's examination may uncover an underlying disorder that can be treated.

CAUSES OF YOUR INSOMNIA

If you have a good idea of the wide range of possible causes of insomnia, you multiply the likelihood of zeroing in on your problem. The line-up of common and uncommon, simple and stubborn, obvious and not so clearly evident reasons suggests a lengthy registry of life's ups and downs. To name only a few:

- caffeine
- noise
- irregular hours
- job stress
- money worries
- pain
- depression
- alcohol
- medications

From such an inventory, you can see at a glance that there may be many starting points for your sleepless nights. It is, no doubt, useful to pinpoint the causes of your insomnia from such a list. But you may be doing a disservice to yourself if you overlook the drawbacks of that kind of roll-call presentation. Consider these:

You are tempted to regard the source of your insomnia as its only cause. It usually isn't. For example, if, as just suggested, you have been warned that with a mid-day nap you are stealing hours from night time sleep, you might be tempted to eliminate your nap. Goodbye insomnia. This approach may work. If your nap, however, is a reaction to boredom, or if it is a part of changing sleep patterns typically found as you grow older, you may not root out your insomnia simply by attacking your nap.

You may have been taking antianxiety (tranquilizer) medication to make it through the day—and night. You have found your abilities to perform on the job, to relate to others, and to sleep at night dissolving. You are tempted to take more medication. But this kind of misuse of mood-altering drugs may prevent your effectively coping with your own situation—high stress exposure at work or fear of unemployment, for example—and, in addition, the drugs may well obscure the basic source of your anxiety. This anxiety may be the source of your insomnia.

The answer to your stress is clearly not indefinite ongoing use of drugs, with all their potential for serious side effects. To stop suddenly, however, may pave the path for a drug-withdrawal insomnia. Even if you are developing more effective means to manage the stresses in your life and rid yourself of the disabling sleeplessness, you may face insomnia from another source—your medication.

In other words, it is all too easy to lock insomnia into a cause-and-effect relationship. It is reasonable to hope that with the cause gone, you can at last sleep. Sometimes this is so, but more often it is not.

You may overlook underlying causes. Perhaps the most compelling reason to understand your insomnia in more than just one dimension is that accepting a one-cause explanation usually leads to treatment that is both inadequate and unsuccessful.

This is not to say that caffeine or a noisy neighbor, for example, cannot be the legitimate, real, and only cause of your sleepless nights. Either may be. But trying to isolate one particular cause can obscure another problem that may not be so easy to uncover.

For example, anxieties about a career. Nagging and weighty worries may contribute to sleeplessness, but they don't magically dissolve on being acknowledged or pointed out. The insomnia may be evidence of the need to develop more workable coping strategies, with perhaps more supportive help of friends, family, and more involvement in some nurturant activities, such as school, church, or hobbies.

Or consider the subject of aging. You may be surprised to find out that the aging process doesn't automatically mean you sleep less. Some people sleep more than they did when younger. Whereas changing sleep-wake patterns are a universal experience of aging, insomnia doesn't always have to follow. Other factors may be responsible for your insomnia—such as a medical problem.

The younger person is not immune to medical illness, but more often it is the older person who suffers chronic medical problems that can disturb sleep. For example:

- gallbladder disease
- alcoholism
- hypertension
- diabetes
- arthritis
- prostate disease

Physical discomfort from illness can trouble sleep. Even a twinge of pain—which may be hardly noticeable when you're awake—can keep you up. With fewer distractions from your surroundings, your attention is more concentrated on the painful condition.

Appropriate treatment of a medical condition may by itself alleviate your insomnia—but it may not. You may be vulnerable to sleep-destroying anxieties and fears over lingering illness, dependency on others, and a feeling of frailty and diminished capacity.

As you grow older, you may find yourself awakening early in the morning, often before dawn. Traditionally, medicine has considered a history of many early-morning awakenings and an inability to fall back asleep—particularly in someone whose sleeping and waking patterns were comfortably balanced—as important clues to a depression. This observation is an oversimplification. Although broken sleep at dawn is a fairly constant symptom in a depressive illness, there are many other possible reasons, such as career changes, pain, marital discord, illness, or reaction to medications.

Older adults, as well, particularly those who have retired or who receive less attention from others, may feel bored, useless, and lost in a youth-oriented culture. They may be inclined to nap during the day, even more than once. If these people go to sleep at their usual time in the evening, they may very likely awaken in the wee hours, such as 4 A.M., feeling as if they had enough sleep.

Cataloging the causes of insomnia often ignores the length of time—days, weeks, months?—you've had yours. Consider the catch-all causes of "worries" or "anxieties" or "stress." A deadline at work, for example, or an unbalanced budget, or even anticipation of a happy event, such as a graduation, may give rise to some episodic anxiety. This response is probably normal and appropriate, even if such worries keep you awake. The important key is how long. In a temporary insomnia, using three to four weeks as a yardstick, your sleeplessness is an understandable, self-limited reaction.

Occasionally, however, insomnia that begins over a temporary situation can become a long-term habit. You may find yourself caught in a cycle of sleepless nights because you fear being unable to fall asleep. It seems the harder you try, the more wide awake you become.

Last, most reasons for insomnia are subtly woven into the fabric of your life. To be understood as a reflection of you, your sleeplessness, and the causes of it, may require you to reassess yourself. The ability to handle the complexities in your life—confronting the alternatives and making decisions—is a learnable skill that can make the difference between a good night's sleep and sleeplessness.

Consider, for example, the complaint of insomnia of a young corporate manager of an investment banking organization. An explanation of the many causes of his sleeplessness should take into account the patterns of a given society. Currents of social change are important and practical considerations, not only for the behavior of a particular person but for the kind of medical treatment offered to an insomniac.

For a member of the "baby boom" generation born in the 1950s—particularly executives on the fast track of business society—the roots of insomnia have become tangled. For example, many baby boomers are casual about drugs. These young adults have used street drugs recreationally for years—marijuana during school days, cocaine in the privacy of the home or office. This fly now—pay later attitude about drugs is a pervasive philosophy, especially in the arena of a medical condition such as insomnia. It is not surprising to find that such a person is favorably disposed toward pills. He or she is as unconcerned about taking sleep medication—be it prescription or over-the-counter—as about snorting coke. It is unlikely that the naive bravado of this behavior will bring on restful sleep. It is certain that the illusion of what will be a brief chemical panacea complicates an already complex situation:

- Insomnia may worsen with sleep medication.
- Sleep medication taken with a diet of other mood-altering drugs—especially depressants, such as alcohol and tranquilizers—is a recipe for accidental overdose and possible death.
- Central nervous system stimulants, such as cocaine and amphetamines, and depressants, such as the antianxiety drugs, can cause by themselves insomnia and fatigue, among other effects.

These apparently contradictory terms—stimulants and depressants—need clarification. "Stimulants" is a description given to a group of drugs—such as alcohol, amphetamines, cocaine, and lookalike diet pills. Just as often, such pills are called "depressants." Which is accurate? Each, depending on the context.

For example, stimulants usually create an initial feeling of excitement, alertness, and heightened cheerfulness. With continued taking of the drug a second stage is reached during which the "euphoria" escalates. In a third stage, as the effects wear off there is a feeling of depression. This depression may be severe enough to trigger suicide.

Further abuse of such stimulants/depressants worsens the swing-high/swing-low effect, as the body tolerates high doses. Psychological dependence occurs, with a binge pattern of stimulation followed by depression, sleep deprivation, and a search for sleep through higher doses of sleep medication.

Peer pressures, and the tensions of our times that produce psychological distress, pose dilemmas that perhaps can be most readily described as the human condition. Looked at in this larger light, the point of decision has profound implications: How can we know if such suffering should be treated with medication, by counseling, or managed alone?

·2·
SLEEPING PILLS:
GREAT EXPECTATIONS

It's no secret that in today's society sleeping pills and other mood-altering substances are consumed in staggering amounts—not only by many people, but continuously for long periods. What this means in terms of how we as a society tolerate some of the afflictions of our age and existence—pain, tension, anxiety, depression, insomnia—is certainly a question worth addressing philosophically. Practically, however, the observation that so many people use sleep medication demands attention: Are sleeping pills safe? Do they work? Do YOU need them?

PILLS FOR YOUR ILLS?
DO SLEEPING PILLS WORK?

Yes, for most people sleeping pills do work temporarily. But you pay a high price. For example:

- After the first few weeks, the effect of the medication may begin to wear off.
- You have a tendency over time to take more medication to get the original effect, with the likely development of dangerous dependence and addiction.
- People who are pill-dependent often do not know it.
- All sleeping pills act on your central nervous system—reducing such basic processes as breathing and vision, along with causing lessened alertness and blunted reflexes.
- You risk, in some cases, developing a temporarily worse insomnia when you stop the pills—a boomerang effect called rebound insomnia.
- Some sleep medications accumulate in your body to an amount where you may have a hangover feeling for several days.
- Some drugs may interfere with the actions of other medications you may be taking.
- You may experience more nightly awakenings and an uncomfortable feeling of not having slept enough.

Insomnia is a symptom, not an illness. Many considerations underlie the symptom of sleeplessness—physical, such as arthritis; psychological, such as loss of a job; environmental, such as night-shift work. The ability to recognize these alternative factors—the causes of your insomnia—is the first step in coping with your sleeplessness. Reliance on sleeping pills eventually will compromise not only your self-esteem and the freedom of your behavior—for dependency lurks just around the corner—but also jeopardizes the success of your efforts toward a good night's sleep.

WITH THESE RISKS, WHY DO SO MANY PEOPLE TAKE SLEEPING PILLS?

Despite all the risks, many people take sleeping pills. Why? For one thing, to many people sleeping pills represent a quick, easy nighttime exit from some of life's daytime troubles. Relief seems to be a swallow away. Many people take many pills for all kinds of ailments, and a sleeping pill—with familiarity— seems like just another pill.

Thousands of people make their first acquaintance with these medications as patients in a hospital or nursing home. In *The Sleeping Pill* (1978), Ernest Hartmann, M.D., a renowned sleep researcher, pointed out that the medical chart for close to half of all adult hospital admissions will include a prescription for sleeping pills.

A large number of people begin taking sleeping pills on the well-meaning advice of their physician who writes, in good faith, a prescription intended for a short period. In an editorial in the *Journal of the American Medical Association* in 1977, Quentin Regestein, M.D., of the Peter Bent Brigham Hospital in Boston, commented:

Often, on complaining of sleeplessness, a patient promptly receives a prescription for hypnotics. [Hypnotics are medications used to promote sleep. They have no connection with hypnotism. (ed. note)] Once regular use of hypnotics begins, giving them up becomes arduous. Regular use of hypnotics might be

more reasonable were they more than temporarily effective . . .
The patient relying on hypnotics is often left with his original
insomnia plus a drug problem.

For many people, pills and other substances—caffeine, nicotine, food additives, alcohol—are part of everyday life. Like
the air you breathe, the more commonplace and ordinary
something is, the less noticeable it becomes. Pills are small,
deceptively simple, and have become a casual, almost universal vehicle of medication. Some contain a mild-acting medication; others contain chemicals so potent that they may be
lethal if mishandled. If you must take sleeping pills, the point
is to take them seriously . . . and just as important, take them
knowledgeably. At the very least, you should know the name
of the medication, why you are taking it, your dosage requirements, and possible side effects.

IS A TRANQUILIZER THE SAME AS A SLEEPING PILL?

Strictly speaking, no. A tranquilizer has a calming effect without producing sleep or heightening alertness. When used to
lessen anxiety, however, a tranquilizer may pave the way for
sleep.

This question of names needs some explanation. The large
number of names can be bewildering. There are chemical
names and brand names for the same substances, as well as
names that are synonyms for that substance. Drugs are often
named by what they do. For example, hallucinogens cause
hallucinations. Sometimes drugs are named according to their
chemistry, such as barbiturates (barbituric acid). Most familiar
are names invented for trademark purposes.

Consider the possible misunderstanding when even a very

widely used medication, triazolam, can be referred to by these names:

• WHICH NAME TO USE? •

Halcion	A brand name or trademark, the label used by the pharmaceutical manufacturer to market the drug
Triazolam	A chemical, or generic, name for Halcion
Benzodiazepine	The name of the chemical family to which Halcion belongs
Sleeping pill	An everyday reference to a popular prescription sleep medication.

The important point to make is that there is no single basic pill which is the universal biochemical yardstick of a sleeping pill. All pills used to bring on sleep cannot yet target the specific areas of the brain that are involved. They instead dampen, or depress, the entire central nervous system. It is an imperfect science at best.

Having said there is no basic substance that is a "sleeping pill," you may wonder what all those substances on the market that are prescribed or taken for sleep are. This is a reasonable question. After all, there has been a worldwide increase in the use of tranquilizers, sedatives, and other antianxiety agents. These substances are part of a large varied group of medications that affect the central nervous system. You may have heard them called mood-altering drugs, or psychotropics, or psychoactives. When used to bring on sleep, such drugs are called hypnotics.

HYPNOTICS

It's easy to be led off track with the word "hypnotic." After all, hypnosis is a state of selective concentration—a trance. It is a technique, not a drug. The general term "hypnotic" refers to those drugs taken to promote sleep. In the field of psychoactive drugs—all those medications that affect the central nervous system—almost every drug is potentially a hypnotic. That is, at a specific dose they can almost all bring on sleep. Two points need to be made about this term:

- One, this use of the term "hypnotic" is not related to the practice of hypnosis.
- Two, the term "hypnotic" is often used interchangeably with the terms sedative and tranquilizer. Drugs so labeled, as well as antidepressants or even antihistamines, are sometimes called hypnotics if used to bring on sleep.

The point to keep in mind is this: A sleeping pill has many faces. Your doctor may conversationally call it a sleeping pill. A pharmacist may describe it as a benzodiazepine or, more specifically, for example, lorazepam. The prescription label probably carries the trademark name, Ativan. Indeed, the overlapping side-by-side names can all refer to one and the same pill.

The following groupings will help you recognize and identify the various names used to refer to sleep medication.

THE NAME GAME

• PSYCHOACTIVE DRUGS COMMONLY • USED FOR INSOMNIA GROUPED BY CHEMICAL FAMILY

Benzodiazepines

Diazepam (Valium)*
Chlordiazepoxide (Librium)
Lorazepam (Ativan)
Oxazepam (Serax)
Flurazepam (Dalmane)
Triazolam (Halcion)
Temazepam (Restoril)

Barbiturates

Secobarbital (Seconal)
Amobarbital (Amytal)
Pentobarbital (Nembutal)
Phenobarbital (Luminal)

Nonbarbiturate-nonbenzodiazepine

Glutethimide (Doriden)
Methyprylon (Noludar)
Ethchlorvynol (Placidyl)
Chloral hydrate (Noctec)

Antihistamine

Over-the-counter sleep aids

*Trademark names appear in parentheses.

If you feel you're getting lost in the nomenclature, here are the key facts:

- All sleep medications—hypnotics—are psychoactive (mood-altering) drugs.
- Sleep medications may be widely different from each other chemically, but their actions have the same effect: They depress the central nervous system—a process on a spectrum ranging from relief of anxiety, suppression of inhibitions, sedation, sleep, and even general anesthesia.
- In high enough doses by themselves, or in combination with other substances, such as alcohol, hypnotic drugs can be lethal.

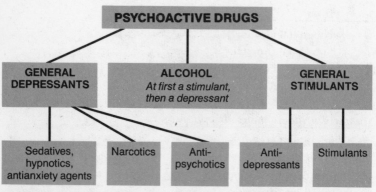

Depressants diminish nervous system activity on a spectrum from relaxation... to sleep... to anesthesia... to coma... and, potentially, death.

Depressants diminish nervous system activity on a spectrum from relaxation . . . to sleep . . . to anesthesia . . . to coma . . . and, potentially, death.

CAN I BUY SLEEPING PILLS WITHOUT A PRESCRIPTION?

Yes, you can buy sleeping pills without a prescription if you interpret a "sleeping" pill as a "drowsiness" pill. Those sleep medications bought over-the-counter—meaning without a prescription—are usually part of a class of drugs called antihistamines. You are probably acquainted with them as they are used mainly to treat "common colds" and some allergies. The drowsiness these pills bring on is a side effect, which is welcomed by the user as the main purpose. Drawbacks to buying these drugs over-the-counter are several:

Casual Use

The wide availability of these drugs in supermarkets, pharmacies, and drugstores, and the ease with which they can be purchased, may leave the mistaken impression that they can be used casually. Pregnant and nursing women, machine operators—even operators of kitchen appliances—drivers, anyone requiring alertness on the job, and anyone taking other medication should not use these drugs without a physician's guidance.

Accidental Poisoning Because of Careless Self-medication

You may not realize you're taking your medication improperly:

- If you don't read the instructions on the package
- If you don't understand or heed details, such as "with meals" or "before meals"
- If you have the mistaken belief that you don't have to be as careful with these medications as with prescription drugs

THE MEDICATION INFORMATION GAP—YOUR NEED TO KNOW

You've probably heard of a managerial method for determining who in an organization gets classified or confidential documents—it's called the "need to know." Health information isn't a military or industrial secret. Yet much of what you need to know during treatment is not as easily accessible as, say, a telephone book. For example, diet and weight-loss programs depend on your ability to steer a path through nutrition choices and calorie lists.

Is this much ado about nothing? After all, how you take medication appears on the surface rather easy—you simply swallow it then and there, with whatever liquid chaser is around. A few of the unrecognized consequences of this action include:

- Possible interactions with other medications or food may prevent efficient absorption of your pill.
- Contraindications—who shouldn't take this medication—may be overlooked.
- Unwanted reactions such as ringing in the ears or hallucinations may not be reported or linked to an action of your medication.

Recent studies have shown that up to 50 percent of all prescription medications are not taken properly. Clearly, the patients' "need to know" doesn't seem to have been met. Consider this further evidence from Food and Drug Administration and American Medical Association surveys:

- Approximately 75 percent of patients given new prescriptions reported not learning about the precautions they should observe.

- Nearly 66 percent of those patients were in the dark about possible adverse side effects.
- 96 percent of patients admitted to not asking any questions at all about their prescriptions—leading their physicians to believe that their patients were adequately informed.

Evidently, the medication communication gap is real: There is a shaky bridge between the patient and the health-care professionals—doctors, nurses, pharmacists, specialized therapists, and health educators.

To help you bridge the gap, a number of professional organizations, voluntary health associations, publishers, and government agencies have developed multimedia instructional materials. These range from newsletter mailers to films, slides, and videotapes. Ideally, according to the National Council on Patient Information and Education, these teaching/learning tools should spotlight and clarify medication questions in five basic areas:

- Name/purpose
  What is the name of my medication? What is it supposed to do?
- Timing
  How and when do I take it, and for how long? These are the practical, humble details that are usually left out of most instructions. For example, do I take the medication before or after a meal? With fruit juice, milk, water, or how?
- Forbidden fruit
  What foods, drinks, other medicines, or activities should I avoid while taking this drug?
- Side effects
  Are there any side effects? Are these common? What do I do if they occur?
- Information/instructions
  Is there any detailed written information already available

about the drug? The answer to this question is yes. There are several medical pharmacology reference books, among which the most widely referred to and found in libraries are:

The Pharmacological Basis of Therapeutics, edited by Louis Goodman and Alfred Gilman. New York: Macmillan, 1985.

AMA Drug Evaluations, fifth edition. Chicago. American Medical Association, 1983.

United States Pharmacopeia. Rockville, Md.: The Pharmacopeial Convention, 1985.

Physicians Desk Reference. Oradell, N.J.: Medical Economics Company, 1986.

These books are highly technical and are intended as global reference sources for experts equipped with a background in biochemistry, physics, and human physiology. Nevertheless, you can gain some practical information about:

- Indications for drugs (who should take this medication?)
- Contraindications (who shouldn't take this medication?)
- Side effects (usually minor, transient discomforts, such as drowsiness, dizziness, dry mouth, constipation, diarrhea)
- Adverse effects (possibly serious; indicate medication should be stopped immediately; report your reaction to your doctor)
- Dosage forms; strengths of doses; special storage conditions. The *Physicians Desk Reference* has color pictures of dozens of medications.

The bottom line you should aim for when you tap a reservoir of information is simply:

To learn enough from your reading to help you frame any questions for your doctor

To understand that most therapy means a change in your behavior and a reorientation of how you view your problem. As a start, for example, this may mean withdrawing from sleep medication and adopting drug-free relaxation techniques to overcome insomnia.

SLEEPING PILLS AND ALCOHOL

I DON'T NEED A SLEEPING PILL— I JUST TAKE A LITTLE SHERRY BEFORE I GO TO BED

A tense person may be relaxed by an ounce of wine. If your drinking stays as restrained as that, and if your liver and kidneys are healthy, you're probably not going to be harmed by one nightly glass of wine.

This view of alcohol, however, masks the reality of its use as a liquid sleeping pill and ignores these facts:

- Alcohol is a psychoactive drug that will depress the central nervous system—like a sleeping pill. For many, it is risky to consider it simply a social mealtime beverage.
- The legal availability of alcohol almost everywhere promotes widespread acceptance and camouflages the dangers of tolerance, dependency, and addiction.
- Alcohol use can disturb the quantity and quality of sleep— even months or years after giving up alcohol.
- Alcohol exaggerates the actions of many commonly used medications and can make the use of an otherwise relatively safe drug dangerous.

IF I STOP MY SLEEPING PILLS OVER THE WEEKEND, CAN I HAVE A COCKTAIL SATURDAY NIGHT?

If you have been taking sleep medication all week long, particularly a long-acting sleeping pill such as flurazepam (Dalmane), you will have accumulated in your body a reservoir of the drug. In other words, there are enough of the active components of your sleep medication still in the bloodstream to have an additive effect when combined with alcohol. An innocently small amount of a prescribed sleeping pill, or an otherwise "safe" medication, has sent many people to the emergency room with a potentially lethal overdose, simply because a few hours earlier they had had several cocktails.

In combining alcohol and sleep medication, you run these risks:

- If this medication is a psychoactive drug—for example, a sleeping pill—you may very well, in all innocence, have pulled the biological trigger on yourself. Vital functions— such as breathing and heartbeat—that have already been changed by alcohol are depressed further toward disaster.
- Alcohol blunts critical judgmental safeguards against taking too many pills. You can easily lose track of what you've taken. Disorientation can last many hours—even through a hangover the next morning.

The deadly consequences of the alcohol–sleeping pill mix become headlines when movie stars or popular entertainers are the victims. Less well recognized are the thousands of people who unknowingly misuse medication legitimately prescribed by physicians or dentists. The average medicine cabinet contains about two dozen drugs. This, combined with the liquor cabinet, constitutes hazardous potential. People who are unaware of the danger of alcohol-pill combinations may thoughtlessly contribute to their own drug abuse.

TOLERANCE, DEPENDENCY, ADDICTION

ABUSE IS UP TO YOU

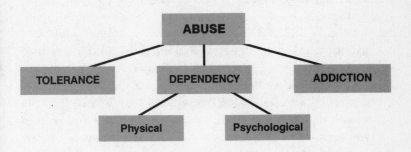

Few people knowingly abuse prescription medication. The fact that abuse occurs so commonly is a commentary on the dearth of information and the mass of misinformation people bring to this subject.

There are three important progressive signposts to abuse: tolerance, dependency, and addiction:

Tolerance

If you need more and more of a medication to achieve the original effect—that's tolerance. Your body has begun to develop resistance to the drug's effects. It's the first stage of a drug problem. In most cases, if you are tolerant to one kind of drug—for example, a sleeping pill in the benzodiazepine family—you will similarly have a tolerance to the other drugs in that family. Here's a fact most people don't know: If you have developed a high tolerance to alcoholic beverages, you may also be tolerant to many of the commonly used sleeping pills.

Dependency

Dependency is defined in two ways—physical dependency and psychological dependency. This terminology is not as tweedle-dee and tweedle-dum as may appear; the choice of the clinically accurate diagnosis can determine a clinically effective treatment.

- Psychological dependency is characterized, in the words of Dr. Kathleen Foley, director of the Pain Clinic, Cornell University Medical College, by "craving a drug for other than pain relief, and becoming overwhelmingly involved in the use and procurement of the drug." *(Pain: Mechanisms and Management,* 1982) A psychological need for mood-changing substances can be seen when pills are taken habitually to help cope with ordinary everyday frustration, disappointment, tension, and insomnia.

- Physical (biochemical) dependency means that the body requires the drug to function normally, for you to feel okay. Most sleeping pills and narcotic painkillers can produce a physical dependency, often revealed only when the drug is stopped suddenly—when the extremely unpleasant withdrawal symptoms surface, such as agitation, tremor, and insomnia.

Addiction

The term "addiction" can be confusing. Some experts state that addiction occurs only when there is an overpowering craving for a substance. This definition links addiction with psychological dependency. Addiction appears to depend on the degree of psychological need.

The existence of an addiction is a kind of biological slavery. The user will feel out of control and overwhelming involvement and compulsion in the continued use and procurement of the drug, despite the most adverse circumstances.

If you are using cocaine, for example, and can stop using it, then you may be dependent on it, but not addicted. However, if you can't stop—that's addiction.

THE ABUSE MYTHOLOGY: ONLY STREET-CORNER TYPES . . .

If you think that because you don't use heroin, cocaine, or other illegal substances or participate in the recreational drug scene you are immune to drug abuse, look again. Here are some facts that democratize the situation:

- With time and usage, everyone may be a potential drug abuser, chiefly through ignorance of the tolerance and dependency possibilities of even the most innocently and legally obtained medications.
- There isn't a safe medication—all have the potential to be abused, if you use them repetitively for a long enough time. This is particularly true of all the psychoactive medicines, among which are your sleeping pills.
- Ten percent of the population is so drug sensitive that for them even small doses can lead to drug dependency and addiction.
- Dependency problems with one kind of pill can mean trouble up and down the same chemical "family." In other words, you can be sensitive to the chemistry of a pill you've never taken.

RECOGNIZING THE PROBLEM

According to the New York State Chemical Dependence Services Unit, pill dependency is an illness that can develop into a serious problem without your realizing it. The need can be physical, or emotional, or both. Some symptoms of prescription drug dependency include:

- Taking sleeping pills every day for more than a week
- Going to two or more doctors for the same medication
- Taking increased amounts of pills to achieve the same effect
- Feeling the need to take pills to make life more bearable
- Considering pills to be more important than people
- Taking pills to avoid withdrawal
- Continuing to take pills even though the medical reason for starting the medication is no longer present
- Insisting on obtaining a prescription for a particular tranquilizer or painkiller

WITHDRAWAL
STOPPING YOUR SLEEPING PILLS

The idea that the shortest distance between two points is a straight line doesn't hold true when withdrawal from sleeping pills is the goal. Actually, the long way around may be the shortest way home. Specifically, abruptly stopping sleeping pills—the short way—is a method that in drug parlance is called quitting "cold turkey."

- Unpleasant, occasionally very serious symptoms—tremors, nausea, rapid heartbeat, diminished sexual capacity for males, even convulsions—can develop following abrupt withdrawal from medication.

- The drug doesn't stop having an effect on your body after you've stopped taking the pills. Your body had subtly adjusted to living with the drug and will react uncomfortably to its sudden disappearance from the bloodstream.

The tempo of medication withdrawal—how fast or how slowly you taper off—can make all the difference between a painful process and a tolerable treatment program.

People take sleeping pills in many different settings. Personal control over medication schedules will differ for those in nursing care and retirement facilities, hospitals, and for those at home. Each person, however, can make sleeping pill withdrawal a realistic goal. If you are guided by these two thoughts, you're on your way: Don't stop cold turkey, and don't go it alone.

THE LIMITS OF SELF-HELP. DON'T GO IT ALONE

Self-treatment is an attractive idea because you are determining in an important way how you want to live. Realistically, however, weaning yourself from powerful psychoactive chemicals you've come to depend on is risky to do alone. Because of potentially hazardous withdrawal reactions and the temptation to go back on to pills, it is advisable to have professional review and monitoring of sleeping pill withdrawal, particularly if:

- You are taking multiple medications and have illnesses such as glaucoma, hypertension, prostate disease, peptic ulcers, or a chronic breathing problem.
- You use alcohol. The multiplier effect alcohol has on sleep-

ing pills exposes you to a whole list of risks, including that emergency room commonplace, overdose injury or fatality.

- Your prevailing mood is an exaggerated high—or a deep low—thereby distorting your ability to make accurate judgments.

- You are pregnant, thinking of becoming pregnant, nursing a baby, or are under medical care for other reasons.

STOPPING GRADUALLY

Almost always, the pace of withdrawal from prescribed sleep medications should be a gradual, stepwise reduction in the amount of sleep medication you are taking. This plan needs to be open to change, depending on how you react at each step. For example, in the early stages, insomnia frequently is a disturbing side effect as your body adapts to even a small dosage reduction. The stepwise plan helps you to accustom yourself to taking less of the drug and also gives you an opportunity to discuss your progress with your physician. If you find that you are experiencing too many withdrawal aftereffects, such as irritability, sleeplessness, dizziness, vivid dreams, or blurred vision, your physician may vary the treatment plan.

These withdrawal experiences are troubling at their least, and dangerous at their most. As Mark Twain used to write on his Mississippi River maps: "Consult local pilot." Your physician is your local pilot. Don't go it alone.

CUTTING BACK. HOW MUCH?
HOW QUICKLY?

The tempo of withdrawal and the amount of sleep medication you subtract from your dosage schedule are key factors in a withdrawal program. There are many formulas. Here are some typical plans that your physician might use:

- Reduce your dosage by one "therapeutic dose" every fourteen days. A therapeutic dose of flurazepam (Dalmane), for example, is often 30 milligrams.
- Or reduce your daily dosage by half, at two-week intervals, so that instead of 30 milligrams nightly, you will take 15 milligrams.
- Another plan is the "drug holiday." This withdrawal plan is an on-off system. For example, you may take sleeping pills for five weekdays and skip them on the two days of the weekend. An alternative drug holiday is to take a pill only every third day. In this way, you may feel more capable later of getting along without the drug. With less ongoing exposure to the drug, there is less likelihood of quickly developing drug tolerance.

Drug holidays as a method of sleeping pill withdrawal are an example of the concept of "drug-free" days. This experimental system, which has been adopted in several geriatric centers to minimize side effects from multiple medications, requires professional medical monitoring. Routinely eliminating the usual doses—for a day or even two days—of your diuretic, laxative, sleep, hypertension, or cardiac medication may have these benefits:

- You may feel more alert and interested in planned activities.

- You will have more time to devote to areas of your interest if you do not have to wait for a pill from a nurse—who will also have more time for you if he or she isn't dispensing medicine. Those centers that are piloting the "drug-free" days are scheduling a full agenda of movies, lectures, games, exercise, and classes.

There is margin for modification in these plans. For example, the pace of withdrawal can be slowed by stretching it out over a longer period, or the medication dose you have cut back can be further reduced by smaller amounts.

These are stepwise plans. At each step, you can anticipate:

- A discussion with your doctor. You may have some withdrawal symptoms, such as vivid dreams or a stomach upset. Be prepared for a temporary period of troubled sleep. These reactions may require adjusting the dose or changing the medication.
- Reduction in the risk of side effects from medication buildup in your body.
- A financial savings as you take fewer pills.
- A boost in morale as you near your goal of being free of sleeping pills.
- Delight to find that you can sleep better without the pills.

DIVIDING YOUR MEDICATION DOSAGE

Dividing a medication into smaller units for a stepwise withdrawal program can be done more readily if the tablet has been scored—there is a groove down the middle—or the pharmaceutical manufacturer supplies the medication in different forms and strengths. For example, diazepam (Valium) comes in 2 mg, 5 mg, and 10 mg strengths as capsules and tablets, and also as a solution for intramuscular and intravenous injection.

On the other hand, if your medication needs to be further divided and is not scored, and/or doesn't come in prepared dosage forms, then your doctor might ask your pharmacist to prepare a reduced dose for you. The pharmacist can carefully weigh and measure in-between sizes. With a chemical scale and a willingness to help, this can be done in short order.

Your tailor-made prescription is only one of many services today's professional pharmacists offer. In many hospitals, they make consultation rounds with the medical team. With the increasing use of computers, they can be the first to spot changes—such as toxic or incompatible drugs—in your medication profile.

SHORT-ACTING OR LONG-ACTING SLEEPING PILLS

Sometimes your doctor will propose to you a withdrawal plan that pivots on switching to a different sleeping pill, that is, one with a different elimination half-life—one that has a different, longer or shorter, length of action.

Elimination half-life refers essentially to how quickly or slowly a drug can be eliminated from your body. Specifically, elimination half-life is the length of time for 50 percent of a dose to be eliminated or cleared from the body. The technical term half-life is a practical concept in the prescribing of sleeping pills, particularly when discussing short-acting versus long-acting drugs.

Medications are absorbed, stored, and eliminated—that is, metabolized—by your body at different rates. The differences depend not only on the biochemical structure of the drug and the size of your dose but also on you—your weight, health, age. For example, elderly people and those of any age with liver or kidney disease will usually "clear" drugs at a slower rate than the statistically normal healthy young adult.

Compare the half-life of flurazepam (Dalmane) in these four groups (adapted from *AMA Drug Evaluations,* fifth edition):

• DALMANE •
ELIMINATION HALF-LIFE COMPARISON
BY AGE AND SEX

Age/Sex	Half-Life
Young males	74 hours
Elderly males	160 hours
Young females	90 hours
Elderly females	120 hours

With such a spectrum of response—influenced by age and medical factors—no single number of hours can give more than a working approximation of elimination half-life.

SHORT-ACTING OR LONG-ACTING
WITHDRAWAL PLANS

The biological facts of elimination half-life are the basis of a more informed selection of which sleep medication to prescribe for insomnia. These biochemical ABC's can also help determine which drug to switch to—if that is to be the first step in your withdrawal. Because shorter- or longer-acting medication can be a central feature of the withdrawal program, it's worth noting these important points:

- The shorter-acting drugs may be used as the first step in withdrawal. Use of these shorter-acting medications is becoming more common. Because of their rapid elimination from the body, however, you may find that a once-daily dose will not prevent withdrawal symptoms. You may require several daily short-acting doses, with the possible option—if withdrawal symptoms don't abate—of returning to the original longer-acting drug.

- Substituting a short-acting drug (half-life value of five to twenty-four hours) for a long-acting drug (half-life value greater than twenty-four hours) can be carried out safely only by a physician.

- The dynamics of a short-acting pill. In many cases, particularly with pills with a very short half-life, active ingredients are metabolized so quickly that you may feel you need more and more to maintain sleep. In fact, by the last part of the night, little or no short-acting drug is left in the bloodstream. As the short-acting drug is cleared from the blood, you may commonly experience an early-morning insomnia—an effect mimicking a cold-turkey withdrawal. This kind of drug-induced insomnia may happen even after only one or two nights on a short-acting pill, and may very well tempt you to increase your dose to stay asleep.

  The pattern seems clear: With a drug that has a rapid elimination half-life—that is, a short-acting one—you may give in to what you may feel as a need for more medication, leading to increased tolerance and likely dependency.

- The dynamics of a long-acting pill. The major benefit of a long-acting sleep medication is, temporarily, lengthened sleep. The major drawback is residual drowsiness. The grogginess can last for several days.

Whereas clinical judgment must weigh and balance the risks and benefits of shorter-acting and longer-acting sleep medications, you may compare for yourself what some of the practical implications of elimination half-life are:

• ELIMINATION HALF-LIFE COMPARISON •

Short-Acting Drugs (e.g., Ativan, Halcion)	*Long-Acting Drugs* (e.g., Valium, Dalmane)
During administration and also during withdrawal, not enough medication is left in the bloodstream to provide a gradual elimination. Intense effects can include worsening of sleeplessness, tenseness, and possible dependency.	Active ingredients accumulate in the bloodstream for days—tolerance prevents the development of overwhelming sedation. These drugs continue to circulate, even after the last dose is taken, with a gradual tapering off of their effects.
Drug tolerance potential—taking more and more to get the original effect—is higher than with longer-acting medication.	Withdrawal effects after a relatively brief, short-term use are infrequent and minimized, with little rebound insomnia. Delayed appearance of sleeplessness—two weeks after stopping—can occur. Hangover effect includes daytime sedation, drowsiness, poor daytime functioning, and mental impairment with confusion in the elderly.

WITHDRAWAL REACTIONS

If you have decided to stop using sleeping pills, you should know that recent research has linked drug withdrawal—and in particular abrupt sleeping pill withdrawal—to a number of uncomfortable reactions. These reactions cover a spectrum from mild to severe, and may include:

- tremors
- insomnia
- dizziness
- convulsions
- irritability
- vivid dreams and nightmares
- stomach upsets

It is an unhappy paradox that the self-same medication designed to relieve your insomnia can be a cause of sleeplessness after its withdrawal. This paradox was at the heart of two related clinical syndromes that were found to follow sleeping pill withdrawal. Here is what the studies have shown:

Rebound Insomnia

While insomnia is insomnia to most of us, the possible worsening of sleep following abrupt sleeping pill withdrawal may actually be a temporary drug-withdrawal reaction. In particular, research studies have suggested that special culprits in this kind of reaction are benzodiazepine drugs. The sleeping pill you're trying to stop taking is very likely a member of this popular drug family.

Rebound Anxiety

Rebound anxiety often accompanies rebound insomnia, and vice versa. If you have rebound insomnia, you may feel agitated and anxious about it during the day; or if you're anxious about your withdrawal program, you may not be able to sleep well at night. Your concern about being able to get along without the fragile crutch of your sleeping pill is only natural.

Rebound insomnia and rebound anxiety may be such a distressing experience that you are tempted to seek relief at any cost. Instead of stopping the drug, you may try to quell the insomnia and rebound symptoms by self-medicating and upping the dosage. The irony is that you become accustomed to the drug and need more of it to create the same effect—a habit-forming condition known as drug tolerance. Eventually, drug dependency—a biochemical or psychological need for a substance—insidiously develops.

Withdrawal is not a simple step. It is, actually, a complex biological change that is influenced as much by the particular individual taking the pill—his or her age, health status, stress exposure, vulnerabilities—as it is by the specific withdrawal program selected.

If you keep in mind that forewarned is forearmed, you can approach your withdrawal program more equably and confidently. Your best insurance of reaching your goal of a drug-free outcome—with the least amount of distress—is:

- Completing a carefully paced, stepwise withdrawal program.
- Realizing that you may experience some disagreeable symptoms. It helps to know that not only is such discomfort temporary, but you and your doctor can minimize that possibility by fine-tuning your withdrawal plan as you go along.

If the technicalities of short-acting and long-acting sleeping pills, elimination half-life, and stepwise withdrawal plans leaves you with a bit of information overload, it may help to remember:

- Your goal is freedom from insomnia.
- Sleeping pills may have been taken in pursuit of this goal—particularly for a transient sleeplessness—but they invariably become part of the insomnia problem.
- Your success in withdrawing from sleeping pills—a reflection of your goal of eliminating insomnia—goes hand in hand with an individualized program of nondrug therapies. Such treatment, ranging from immediate changes (such as more regular bedtimes) to more long-range efforts at managing stressful events in your life, is a basic key both to overcoming insomnia and withdrawing from sleeping pills.

SLEEPING PILL WITHDRAWAL IN THE OLDER ADULT

With the so-called graying of society, particularly in the United States, the likelihood of many older people being labeled "senile" rises dramatically. This sometimes pejorative word is frequently directed at those who are neither senile nor for that matter elderly. The truth may be not senility but overmedication.

The term "senile" has been used as a diagnosis or description of people who, for whatever reason, seem confused, mentally impaired, presenting possible memory deficits, and thought disorders. These symptoms, at any age, however, can reflect "hangover" levels of medication in the bloodstream, particularly of those drugs that affect the central nervous system.

The benzodiazepine family of drugs, among which are the most widely taken tranquilizers, sedatives, and hypnotics (sleeping pills), are special offenders in this category, and elderly people, in particular, are their special victims. This is so for several reasons:

A Metabolic Slowdown

The liver and kidneys—the major metabolic clearance centers in the body—generally don't work as quickly or efficiently in the elderly as they do in younger people. Chronic liver and kidney disease compound this difficulty, making the older person with such malfunctions even more sensitive to an "average" medication dose. The average dose among healthy young people is an overdose for many frail elderly people.

Medication Buildup

Accumulation of medication within the body is an insidious process with potentially damaging consequences. All too commonly, older people with multiple chronic conditions—for example, high blood pressure, angina, fluid retention, arthritis, and insomnia—take many pills, and usually have been doing so for months and even years. Not only are the hazards of drug interactions and side effects multiplied among people on complicated medication schedules, but drug buildup poses the greater risk of a bewildered, confused person—someone more likely to mix up medications, forget a dose, or even take the wrong dose—too many or too few doses.

An older adult's slowed-down systems and possible medication buildup mean that sleeping pill withdrawal is a bit more complicated for them than for other age groups. For example:

- During the withdrawal program, dose reduction steps should be smaller.
- The tempo of withdrawal should be slower—a more widely spaced, stretched-out schedule over longer periods of time.

- Close professional monitoring of the withdrawal may be needed, even on a daily basis, if withdrawal symptoms are unusually severe—a possibility for people long accustomed to taking sleep medication.

A medication withdrawal program can be aided by any one of a medically prescribed roster of social activities, such as appropriate exercise, dance classes, and hobby workshops, as well as nondrug relaxation skills and counseling.

THE IDEAL HYPNOTIC?

FROM A TO B: ANXIETY AND ALCOHOL TO BARBITURATES AND BENZODIAZEPINES

The search for a safe and effective sleep potion—the ideal hypnotic—persists. In an era of scientific discoveries, it is still hard to dismiss the ageless observation that "there is nothing new under the sun." After all, the central themes of life, the motifs of a lifetime—love, happiness, sadness, grief—exist, are felt, and have been written of passionately through the ages.

What about that ageless search for an insomnia panacea? A miracle potion that will deliver you into the welcome arms of Morpheus quietly and safely? Isn't there something new under the sun here? The years throughout the centuries reflect the ebb and flow of enthusiasms for various new insomnia therapies.

But over and over, the search for an insomnia cure resembles a Cinderella story told backward. The princess is discovered in her finery, and the tale of happy expectations takes a nose dive from there to reality. Consider, for example, these once-popular hypnotics:

Alcohol

In the nineteenth century, it was accepted and praiseworthy practice to prescribe a decanter of wine to induce sleep, every night, for years. The extensive web of social, religious, medical, and personal use and misuse of alcohol that has evolved has obscured the fact that alcohol is a short-acting drug—and that, far from being insomnia therapy, it can be a killer.

Opiates

The nineteenth century use of opiates led to this observation in the *Official Report of the Medical Officer of the Privy Council* (1869): "To push the sale of opiate . . . is the great aim of some enterprising wholesale merchants. By druggists it is considered the leading article." All narcotics—opium, laudanum, morphine, heroin, codeine—are eventually addicting, with a serious and sometimes fatal withdrawal syndrome.

Cocaine

The central nervous system stimulant cocaine was once—surprisingly—credited as a hypnotic. Included as an ingredient in the original Coca-Cola in the late nineteenth century, cocaine was touted as the cure-all of a long string of problems, including, oddly enough, insomnia. Cocaine is highly addictive psychologically. A profound depression can occur, not only on withdrawal, but during use of the drug.

BARBITURATES

Another Cinderella was born in 1903. The discovery of a new family of drugs—including medication given for sleep, pain relief, and sedation—appeared to promise the end of the search for a chemical miracle, that is, a safe and effective sleep potion. Barbital was introduced under the trade name of Veronal. Derived from barbituric acid, the new drugs—barbiturates—were well accepted. In 1912 phenobarbital was marketed under the name Luminal. The long, long climb from alcohol to opium, laudanum, heroin, morphine, and codeine had led at last to a major mountain peak: the barbiturates.

- The barbiturates had no odor, no taste, and seemingly no addiction potential.
- They were low in cost.
- And they had bona fide medical uses—they were invaluable (and still are) in, for example, the treatment of epilepsy.

So popular were the barbiturates that an estimated billion grains (65 million grams) were taken annually in the United States by the end of the 1930s. The barbiturates seemed to represent the ideal sleeping pill:

- Their effects were apparently quick—they would cause you to fall asleep promptly and stay asleep through the night, without interfering with normal sleep patterns.
- Their use entailed no apparent risk—you could be free from tolerance, dependency, and addiction potential.
- They were apparently safe from possible suicide attempts.
- They had no disagreeable taste or odor and were low in cost.
- They had no apparent morning-after hangover effect.

The question of a morning-after hangover effect is important. The levels in your bloodstream of a psychoactive drug may make you feel lethargic the next day. You may be described as sedated or tranquilized. All in all, to a greater or lesser degree, with a morning-after hangover:

Your state of alertness is compromised.

Your cognitive abilities—your thinking—are diminished.

Your movements are slowed.

By the 1940s, however, the disadvantages and limitations of the barbiturates could not be ignored:

- They caused tolerance and withdrawal symptoms paralleling those of alcohol, such as insomnia, drunken behavior, slurred speech.
- They had a low margin of safety, indicated by the high number of suicides.
- They caused sleep-pattern abnormalities.
- They became "thrill pills"—and a drug that for decades had been used sensibly found its way into the dangerous recreational market. People discovered that taking barbiturates was like drinking alcohol—in short, one became "drunk." The barbiturates came to be thought of as "solid alcohol," and alcohol "liquid barbiturate."

You may be beginning to wonder if there isn't finally something new under the sun for the tormented sleepless.

BENZODIAZEPINES

Enter the royal family of hypnotics. With sales figures in the billions of dollars, these medications were promoted as the answer to a need for—in an increasingly stressful world—a safe and effective antianxiety drug and hypnotic. Indeed, in the early sixties, with the market appearance of diazepam (Valium) and chlordiazepoxide (Librium), it seemed that the ideal sleeping pills had been found:

- First, the drugs were advertised as relatively safe—even a handful of pills wasn't likely to be fatal.
- Second, tolerance to the drug and dependence on it did not appear readily. The user seemed not to need to increase the dose to get the original effect.
- Third, it appeared that the drug was cleared from the body in a relatively short time. No next-day hangover.

For years the benzodiazepine family seemed to be superdrugs, not only encouraging sleep but capable of relaxing muscles, relieving tension, and calming overexcitability.

The wish may have been father to the thought. But the hopes for these apparently miracle drugs could not be sustained in the face of thousands of clinical observations to the contrary. Here are a few:

Insomnia

The paradox is that the drug giving you relief in the beginning surprisingly is responsible for a return of your symptoms after you stop taking it. In a landmark study in the journal *Pharmacology* (1983), Kales and colleagues wrote: "Rebound insomnia is a specific type of withdrawal sleep disturbance identified with benzodiazepine drugs . . . occurs even when the drugs have been administered for short-term periods in a single nightly dose."

In the same study, the authors identified a related syndrome that they called rebound anxiety. Other withdrawal effects can occur as well, even as late as six weeks after the drug is stopped. These effects may include rapid pulse, sweating, nausea, tremor, depression, and convulsions. *The Medical Letter* (May 1, 1981) reported that: "All of these symptoms plus hallucinations and psychosis have also occurred following use of diazepam (Valium) at therapeutic dosage levels . . . usually about three days after the drug was stopped."

Dependency

The presence of withdrawal symptoms suggests a drug dependency. Your body is reacting to your stopping a drug that it had "learned" to live with over a period of time. Studies have shown that people with a history of drug and/or alcohol abuse and those who may be "dependency prone" are often dependent on benzodiazepine drugs. According to the data presented by Ruth Cooperstock in *Society and Medication: Conflicting Signals for Prescribers and Patients* (1983): "Between 33 and 40 percent of patients attending two large treatment centers in Ontario for treatment of alcohol-related problems are reported to be users of and frequently dependent upon benzodiazepines."

If, however, you are on a low-dose, intermittent, or short-term prescription, drug dependency is less likely.

Next-day Hangover

Here is where the booby trap lies for the benzodiazepines. Some of them accumulate in your body for days. You may feel drowsy for a considerable time, not only at night but during the day, depending on the length of time you have taken the drug. You may experience learning and memory deficits as well as diminished alertness and hand-eye coordination. In other words, hard or inconvenient as it may be, try to arrange alternatives to driving a car or taking a test.

OVER-THE-COUNTER DRUGS

When you buy a package of aspirin, you hold a kind of chemical miracle in your hand—a wonder drug whose uses run the gamut from painkiller to sleep aid, and sometimes both at the

same time. The simplicity of the over-the-counter purchase—
with no prescription needed—and the seeming ordinariness
of this drug belie its occasional potential for injury, making
aspirin a kind of model of what you should know about over-
the-counter drugs.

Aspirin wears the cloak of safety. It is often the drug of
choice to relieve a headache and a variety of body pains; and
it can reduce arthritic swelling and fever. Millions of users feel
it can do no wrong.

Yet consider this: There is recent evidence concerning the
relationship between aspirin when used to treat fever in children who have chickenpox or influenza virus infections and
the subsequent occurrence of a life-threatening systemic disorder called Reyes syndrome. The linkage is not proven, or
even understood, but enough of a shadow exists to have triggered nationwide debate about whether mandatory warning
labels should be placed on aspirin packages.

Fortunately, most of the time you can probably take aspirin without a second thought. But it is worth knowing
that aspirin, like any drug, has potential drawbacks, such
as these:

- Aspirin may touch off or exacerbate gastrointestinal ulcers
  and/or bleeding.
- Aspirin may interfere with the body's ability to coagulate
  blood—a natural defense against excessive bleeding.
- Too much aspirin over an extended period may affect the
  central nervous system and cause ringing in the ears.
- Aspirin should be avoided in pregnancy because it may interfere with the defenses against bleeding of both mother
  and fetus.

Aspirin makes a most persuasive example of your need to
be reminded about the consequences of your decision to purchase an over-the-counter medication. The point to the aspirin

story is that even a product which is the most widely used and apparently safe, and which can be purchased anywhere, has risks, just like any other medicine.

What holds for aspirin can be even more true with the nonprescription sleep aids that are so easily purchased over-the-counter by millions of people.

Since the safety and effectiveness of a medication—and over-the-counter preparations are medications—are critical in your selection of a sleep aid, you should know these important facts:

- The active ingredient in the over-the-counter sleep aids is usually an antihistamine.
- The Food and Drug Administration considers these antihistamines to be safe:

  diphenhydramine hydrochloride

  diphenhydramine monocitrate

  doxylamine succinate

  pyrilamine maleate

Millions know the antihistamines as an antidote to symptoms of a runny nose or flu and take them as readily as they take aspirin for headache. But, like aspirin, antihistamines have potential effects that most people don't recognize as hazardous:

- The mental slowdown: inability to concentrate, to focus, or to drive a car underscore the depressant effect of antihistamines on the central nervous system. It is this very side effect—the drowsy, sedativelike action—that people want when they purchase a sleep aid.
- Among other common untoward reactions to the antihistamines are:

ringing in the ears

dizziness

blurred vision

loss of appetite, nausea, vomiting

- At particular risk are persons with asthma, glaucoma, or enlarged prostate.
- The amount of antihistamine in any sleep aid may be too minimal to promote sleep. The boundary between too much and too little antihistamine is the difference between toxicity and comparative safety. It is difficult to formulate just the right balance—too much antihistamine risks toxic symptoms, too little is ineffective for bringing on sleep.
- Drug tolerance to antihistamines is commonplace. If you take more and more antihistamine to achieve the desired drowsiness, you risk self-poisoning.

Over-the-counter sleep aids and a prescription sleeping pill represent the same method of handling insomnia. That method—going straight to a bottle of pills, the "quick fix"—not only may jeopardize your health and mask other underlying conditions, but it also diminishes the opportunity you have of selecting other nondrug alternatives. All drugs have risks—particularly over-the-counter medications, where the ease of purchase and wide availability make them seem as if they are not medicines.

At a time when you need to be clearheaded about treating your insomnia, pills that indiscriminately blanket the central nervous system may pose more problems than they prevent.

OVER-THE-COUNTER SLEEP AIDS

Because of easy availability and the broad media exposure of over-the-counter products, it is important to repeat this caution: The following list is for recognition purposes only. It is not a recommendation for the treatment of insomnia.

Antihistamines

Diphenhydramine hydrochloride (Benadryl, Sominex Formula 2)
Diphenhydramine monocitrate
Doxylamine succinate (Unisom)
Pyrilamine maleate (Nervine, Nytol, Quiet World, Sleep-Eze)

Antihistamine ingredients cause drowsiness. Use only occasionally, and at recommended dosages. They are potentially hazardous for people with glaucoma, asthma, and prostate enlargement. People who use alcohol, are pregnant or nursing, or on other medications are at risk when taking these drugs.

All bromides (ammonium, potassium sodium)

Not recommended as sleep aids. The effective dose for inducing sleep is close to the toxic dose.

Scopolamine

Not recommended as a sleep aid. The safe dose for sleep is too low to be effective. Larger doses are toxic.

DAY-TO-DAY BASIC INFORMATION

GENERIC DRUGS

Every drug has a generic name that is derived from its chemical name. For example, diazepam is the generic name of Valium; flurazepam is the generic name of Dalmane. In the Reader's Guide you will find profiles of some commonly used sleeping pills. The generic name is at the top of each page.

It's worth it to ask for the generic form of the drugs you take. Theoretically, generic medications are less expensive than their trademark or proprietary counterparts. But are they? Sometimes. Pharmacies differ—yours may offer a significant reduction on generic drugs, whereas another pharmacy may not. This latter pharmacy perhaps justifies its higher price structure by convenience services, such as charge accounts, computerized personal drug histories, and the willingness of the registered pharmacist to take the time to answer your questions.

If your doctor suggests sleep medication, you can request a generic prescription. Don't be surprised, however, if your doctor prefers the trademark form. Many physicians stick to trademark drugs they have used for years and whose active and inactive ingredients they are completely familiar with. The higher price, they feel, may represent dependable quality controls and wider manufacturing experience with those rarely mentioned pill components, such as binders, colorings, and emulsifying agents. Most states give physicians the right to prohibit substitution of a generic for a trademark product.

The practical effect of these out-of-sight pill-making factors is how they influence bioavailability. Bioavailability is a characteristic of medication—how efficiently the active ingredient is distributed throughout the body and bloodstream and the predictable span of time necessary for this to occur. With tightened Food and Drug Administration and United States Pharmacopeia standards, differences in bioavailability have been kept to a reassuring minimum.

If your pharmacist is given the discretion to substitute a generic drug for a trademark one—and if the prescription drug is available generically—he or she has on hand lists of acceptable generic substitutes.

A PILL IS A PILL IS A PILL . . .

Many pills are not pills at all, in the sense of a hard tablet. They may be small gelatin capsules. This is not an idle distinction, particularly if you are trying to divide your dosage. For example:

- If you are on a medication withdrawal program and need to cut your dose in half, it is a great convenience if the manufacturer has "scored" the tablet. The word "score" refers to a grooved line cut into the surface of some tablets so that, with a little gentle fingertip pressure, you can break the tablet cleanly in half. Plastic "pill splitters" are often available through mail-order houses.
- A better way to create a more precise fractional dose is to ask your pharmacist whether smaller doses are available, or can be fabricated on your doctor's orders.

These details may appear fussy—indeed, they are fussy—but the difference between a whole dose or half dose can really affect you. Most medications for insomnia are potent depressants of the central nervous system. Some have such a narrow margin for safety that attention to details of how much and how often is important, if not vital. Every little bit of information helps—the color of the capsule or tablet, the container, its cap, the information on the label, and often some patient information in written form.

Check these details, which will help make the taking of medications surer, safer, and more effective for you:

Colors

Both tablets and capsules come in colors. You may think this is much ado about nothing, but doctors frequently hear patients report their daily pill intake like this: "First I take the large blue pill in the morning, then the red tablet, and two green ones for my water. At night, I take the blue one again."

Color coding is a great help in keeping track of your pill intake, particularly if you are taking more than one kind of pill, and doubly so if you have different dosage schedules to remember. Some people can memorize label names of their pills, but for many the colors are easier.

You may question this emphasis on organizing multiple pills, especially if you are concerned with only one nighttime sleeping pill. The fact is that many people—particularly elderly people—take multiple medications. If you are one of these people—or are responsible for one—it's worth taking a few minutes each morning to set up the dosage schedule for the whole day.

Containers

If you buy your medication at a drugstore or pharmacy, it probably comes in a plastic container. By law these containers must meet packaging standards of the Poison Prevention Packaging Act and have child-proof or child-resistant caps. The caps are not only difficult for children to remove—a worthwhile lifesaving feature—but are also almost impossible for many adults to remove. Anyone with arthritic fingers or blood circulation problems in their fingers and hands can tell a tale or two about grappling with these pill bottle caps. Flexible plastic snap-on or screw-on caps are available. Ask your pharmacist to exchange caps for you, if need be, and if there is no danger to anyone in your household.

Labels

Medication labels usually promise more than they deliver. In the little space available, there are several typed names and numbers:

doctor's name

name of the medication

strength of the medication

whether a refill has been approved

The doctor's instructions cannot always be compressed into the space of a small label. Usually what happens is that memory-jogger: "take as directed." The "as directed" phrase raises the issue of doctor-patient communication. Many patients do not remember the details of what the doctor directed them to do, unless they had written it down. For example, do you take the medication with meals, before or after meals? or on an empty stomach? If you're not sure, ask the doctor, nurse, or pharmacist to write the instructions for you. Many doctors use printed patient instruction sheets.

Shelf life or expiration date? A little clarification of these terms is in order to spare you from possible misuse of your medication. The expiration date—which may or may not be printed on the label—refers only to medication in unopened containers. After you open the container, the given expiration date is no longer applicable. The shelf life or true expiration date of medication in an open container is considerably re-duced from the typed or stamped expiration date. For exam-ple, aspirin is particularly sensitive and will deteriorate in heat and humidity—both of which are found in every bathroom or automobile glove compartment.

Always read the label each time you take your medication. This advice is good preventive medicine. Remember these points:

Make sure there's enough light to read the label—don't take your medication in the dark.

Wear your glasses or use a magnifying glass, if necessary.

• PRESCRIPTION PAD ABBREVIATIONS •

Abbreviation	Latin	Translation
a.c.	*ante cibum*	before meals
b.i.d.	*bis in die*	twice daily
c̄	*cum*	with
gr.	*granum*	grain(s)
gtt.	*guttae*	drops
h.s.	*hora somni*	at bedtime
mg	*milligrammum*	milligram(s)
o.d.	*omni die*	each day
p.c.	*post cibum*	after meals
p.o.	*per os*	by mouth
p.r.n.	*pro re nata*	when needed
q.d.	*quaque die*	every day
q.h.	*quaque hora*	every hour
q.i.d.	*quater in die*	four times daily
stat.	*statim*	at once, immediately
t.i.d.	*ter in die*	three times daily

·3·
PRACTICALITIES:
SELF-HELP REMEDIES

Once upon a time in Cleveland, Ohio, an old shoe-maker who had never gone to school taught himself to read and write. In his shop window was a cardboard, hand-lettered sign: "The most helping hand I have is at the end of my right arm." That's where yours is too.

Although it's often difficult to take an arm's-length look at patterns of living you've always taken for granted, the effort is worth it. If you can develop a perspective on how you live, you'll be less likely to bring to bedtime a stew of feelings and tensions that are destructive to sleep. And you may be more apt to flexibly and sensibly modify individual habits—such as going-to-bed times—or creatively adapt the sleeping environment with sleep aids.

SOME COMMON SENSE ABOUT SLEEP

BEDTIMES—HOW REGULAR ARE YOURS?

Falling asleep usually is easier if you have a regular bedtime and wake-up time. Even if you've had a rocky night's sleep, try getting up at your regular time anyway. Of course there are roadblocks to this seemingly simple advice. But these can usually be overcome:

- The kind of work you do—late nights at the office?—and your family life—who's up and about when you're trying to sleep?—often determine your bedtime, as does your temperament. *In Sleep and Wakefulness* (1963), Dr. Nathaniel Kleitman, a leading sleep expert, pointed out that: "Some persons are temperamentally more suited to a regular mode of living than are others. Morning persons have an advantage over evening ones, as the 'early-to-bed early-to-rise' system, upon which the working hours of society are largely based, fits in with their natural inclination."

- It is possible that for many people the day has been artificially extended. Electric lights, television, and the "city that never sleeps" have lengthened our days, shortened the night hours available for sleep, and made less likely a regular bedtime.

- One widespread nightly ritual is the 10 or 11 P.M. television news. For some, this is a wrap-up of the day's dramatic events just before turning out the lights, but for others this parade of the world's problems in living color is hardly a form of presleep relaxation.

RESTLESSNESS

If you've been tossing and turning in bed for a while and sleep evades you, get out of bed and do something else. If you find yourself going to bed not to go to sleep, but to watch television—particularly rousing programs—you risk forming a conditioned reflex in which bed and wakefulness go hand in hand. Avoid forming an association between lying in your bed and unwilling wakefulness. Try an undemanding activity in another room—reading, knitting, solitaire, listening to music—whatever you've found relaxes you.

Consider the possibility that you may be going to bed earlier than you need to. Perhaps you're hoping to recoup lost hours of rest. More hours in bed, however, usually do not lead to sound sleep. In fact:

- You may sleep only half the number of hours you've given yourself for the night.
- You may take longer than thirty minutes to fall asleep.
- You may awaken frequently during the night.

If these are your symptoms, you're spending too much time in bed trying to sleep.

You can aim at making your bedtime hours for sleep count if you:

- Go to bed later—perhaps by one or two hours.
- Try not to nap during the day—you may be sleepy for a while during the first week or so until your nighttime sleep improves. Try not to be discouraged in your efforts to push back daytime drowsiness. Hang in there.
- Get up at the same time in the morning.

This technique avoids fragmentary daytime naps and early bedtimes in favor of consolidating sleep time. By pulling together sleep time into a tighter package, you may help yourself sleep more restfully and for longer periods.

PRESLEEP ROUTINES

In preparing for that long day's journey into night, almost everyone has a bedtime routine—knowingly or not. Yours may be brushing your teeth or reading a book or magazine. Saying prayers is a common nightly practice for many. A nightlight or glasses at the bedside; checking the door locks, the windows, the stove; lowering the thermostat; or turning out the lights may mean the difference between a secure feeling and a sense of something is missing. There's no need to turn these into emotional hangups, but as an end-of-performance curtain—particularly for business and vacation travelers—they provide a practical completion to the day.

DENTAL DETAILS

A common but underrated presleep detail is a bedtime routine for dentures you may be wearing. Sound sleep may seem a long way off from dentures, toothpaste, or mouthwashes. Ill-fitting dentures, however, can be more than an irritating daytime discomfort. Sore gums can keep you up at night. So can a dry mouth—a common cause of poor denture fit. The inside surface of the mouth is covered with tissue as smooth as the tissue inside your lips. That surface is normally maintained by an almost invisible film of lubricating saliva. The loss of some of that liquid film—a frequent side effect of medications such as antidepressants and sleeping pills—leaves an uncomfortable sandpapery feeling. If you are a bit lightheaded from multiple medications, and experiencing repeated dry mouth episodes, you can possibly set up a chain of mouth difficulties that includes:

sore spots along your gums

difficulty in chewing

compromised nutrition

There's no need to press the panic button. Good dental care—the correct fitting of dentures, appropriate and routine cleaning and rinsing—can almost always help your mouth's naturally strong defenses to heal. Dentures are a fact of life for many older people. But particularly for the frail elderly, the benefits of a comfortable mouth and sound dental hygiene may ease nighttime slumber.

NIGHT FOOD

The whole subject of eating and its relationship to sleep is complex. Hunger can disturb sleep. So can a heavy meal. So can caffeine-containing drinks such as coffee, tea, chocolate, and cola, or hard-to-digest foods. If you're hungry, try those standard-bearers of nutrition—warm milk, or a warm wheat or malt-based beverage. (Don't overdo the liquids—you'll risk later awakenings to urinate.) There's little need to feel you are reinforcing wakefulness by rewarding yourself for being awake. If a cracker or a glass of milk or any light snack leaves you feeling satisfied, you may find you can fall asleep without effort.

Milk contains l-tryptophan, which is a natural substance that seems to aid sleep. In 1981, however, in a medical publication, one expert said: "Although side effects and withdrawal symptoms are not present, its (l-tryptophan) effectiveness as a clinically useful sedative drug has not been demonstrated." In *The Sleeping Pill* (1978), Ernest Hartmann, M.D., an expert on the subject of l-tryptophan, has been investigating for decades its effects on sleep and has found that this natural substance (sometimes referred to as a drug when produced by a laboratory) seems to play a biochemical role in sleep mechanisms. At the same time, it is not a general central nervous system depressant. For this reason, and because l-tryptophan reduces sleep latency as well as increasing subjective sleepiness, Dr. Hartmann has suggested that it appeared quite possible that l-tryptophan will turn out to be a safe and useful sleeping pill. In Great Britain, some research has suggested that l-tryptophan has an antidepressant activity, although other studies don't support this claim. L-tryptophan has been marketed there in combination with the B-vitamin pyridoxine. Amidst the pros and cons of this intriguing and hopeful research, you should check with your doctor before giving it a try.

NIGHTCAPS

Alcohol is a two-edged sword. The world seems to be divided into those people who can stop after one drink and others who can't. Most experts suggest avoiding an alcoholic nightcap entirely. In the midst of this debate, certain central facts emerge:

- Alcohol is easily abused. Psychological or biochemical dependency, or both, is a high risk. Alcohol starts off benignly supportive in helping you get to sleep, but you risk enslaving yourself to the tyranny of "just one more drink."

- Laboratory studies have shown that the quality of sleep deteriorates with alcohol. With poorer sleep, the one nightcap may lead to two or more. This is hazardous territory because the tipsy sleeper may unwittingly take sleeping pills.

NIGHTTIME DRAMA

There are a number of bedtime no-nos for anyone afflicted with insomnia. For example, try not to engage in strenuous exercise in the evening—too much, too late is energizing. A good idea—worth repeating—is to refrain late in the day from pick-me-up drinks that contain caffeine. If you're quite sensitive to this stimulant, you probably should cut it out altogether. Last, while not always preventable or under your control, keep your late-evening conversations and discussions friendly. Politics, arguments, and heated exchanges can stall a smooth drop-off for the night.

While any one of these activities may have a place in your life before nightfall, the flow of adrenaline they all cause will not help you sleep. Such get-up and go thwarts the wind-down you need and signals your body that bedtime signs can be ignored.

NAPS

You may be, like Winston Churchill, able to thrive on a short nap in the afternoon. If you have an office couch, if you won't be trounced by your organization, and if you have time, napping may work for you.

On the other hand, you may awaken from a nap feeling

worse than before—tired, grouchy, unrefreshed. You may be cautioned against napping at all and warned that you are stealing hours from nighttime sleep. Perhaps . . . but there are those who find a short nap restorative. For example, if you've been hassled all day long—paperwork, children's schedules, phones ringing, rush-hour traffic—a fifteen-minute nap, even in the late afternoon, can fortify a badly needed equilibrium.

For some, particularly older adults whose sleep-wake patterns are more broken up than before, short siestas are part of their sleep-activity cycle.

Your difficulty sleeping may reflect a feeling that modern times—big brother, big business, big everything—leaves you little room to be captain of your ship and master of your fate. Napping can be a deliberate means to organize your sleep-wake pattern. Taking a siesta may require do-not-disturb signs, taking the phone off the hook, and alerting friends of your time-out.

The point is that daytime napping isn't necessarily a no-no. Naps may be a practical way for you to satisfy your sleep needs. Deciding to include a nap in your day—to catch up on sleep, or to relieve tension—may be a sensible and flexible step to better control your sleep-wake rhythm.

SEXUAL SATISFACTION

The connection between a good night's sleep and your sexuality is less cause and effect than it is one of attitude. The secret is good communication: the need to give and receive physical pleasure and warmth and the ability to express the subtleties and delicacies of your own sexuality. If you welcome this responsibility—to enlighten and reveal your sensitivities and fantasies and to discover those of your mate—chances are that your honesty and openness can be the foundation for refreshing sleep.

Particularly so if you are among the millions who are physically disabled, confined to a wheelchair, or with use of only one arm, or one leg, or crippled by arthritis. The often healthy connection between your sexuality and sound sleep becomes a tenuous thread if you—disabled—consider yourself without sexual rights, without a sexual identity. If you feel inhibited or embarrassed about what you can or can't do, about your visible disabilities, about a catheter, an appliance, a scar, or even a tremor, you may be laying the groundwork for loneliness, tension, and, yes, insomnia.

Sexual pleasure is your choice—it's not as formidable as it seems. The versatility of sexual expression, sexual aids, thoughtful and arousing preparation, and frank discussion of your capabilities with your mate can minimize your anxiety and open the doorway for you to the joys of a satisfying relationship.

CIGARETTE SMOKING

"Don't smoke in bed" is a familiar warning. Accidental fire isn't the only hazard, however. Disturbed sleep is another, particularly for heavy smokers who might crave more cigarettes in the middle of the night, when nicotine withdrawal symptoms can occur. Studies have also shown that heavy smokers generally take longer to fall asleep at bedtime.

JUNGLES OF THE NIGHT: EQUIPPING YOUR SLEEP SAFARI

Sleep gear is remarkable for its variety and practicality. Sleeping aids range over a wide spectrum of bedroom fittings. This list may suggest to you some sensible ideas. Most of the gadgets are widely available, easy to use, and reasonably inexpensive.

EAR PLUGS

Ear plugs block out noise. The wax kind can be molded by finger pressure to fit an individual ear canal, and are disposable. Rubber ear canal plugs are premolded, washable, and reusable. Some people prefer squeezeable foam-rubber plugs. Buy these in sports stores.

FACE MASK

Don't pooh-pooh this simple device. If the mask keeps out the room light that is preventing you from falling asleep, you may have discovered a quick, low-cost solution. Some cleverly designed masks have a special pince-nez, like the nosepiece of an eyeglass frame, to keep them in place. Other masks are washable—a useful feature if you use nighttime facial cosmetics.

WHITE NOISE MACHINE

A "white noise" machine muffles environmental noise. Sound engineers use the term white noise to mean any continuous, low-pitched sound, such as recordings of waves washing the shoreline. A table or floor fan or air conditioner fan does much the same thing, but without the oceanic poetry. Audiocassette voice recordings are also available, usually in the form of a quiet, repetitive exhortation to relax you. Some of these cassettes have an automatic playback feature so that, at the end of the tape, the machine reverses and continues to play again without interruption until an electrical stop point.

PILLOWS

Pillows are a matter of individual comfort. They come in innumerable sizes, shapes, and degrees of plumpness. There was a time when a pillow was a pillow was a pillow—but today's pillows, like almost everything else, are specialized. If you have an allergy, try a pillow filled with a synthetic nonallergenic material rather than with feathers. If you have no allergy problems, you can indulge in a variety of feather-filled pillows—goose down being the most costly. Most pillows are rectangular, but you can find any geometry you want—circles, triangles, cylinders. A pillow with a cut-out space for the neck—crescent-shaped—is often considered indispensable by people with neck arthritis and/or muscle tension. People with certain heart conditions or respiratory problems may find breathing easier if they use two or three pillows. (If you find that you can breathe easier when you use more pillows, discuss this fact with your doctor. A sleep disorder called sleep apnea may be an underlying problem and needs prompt attention and treatment.)

BEDS

You don't have to belong to the nobility to sleep in a king- or queen-size bed, especially if you toss and turn frequently. Sleep research using invisible light—infrared photography—has shown how much sleepers really do move, even those who insist they didn't move a muscle all night. Blankets, sheets, and pillows may be pulled into such helter-skelter disarray that it's hard to surrender to sleep.

Two considerations about royal-size beds are that they need more space and they're costlier to buy and equip with sheets and blankets. But if you find that even the standard double-size bed is too confining, the queen- and king-size beds may be worth the extra cost in sleeping comfort.

Your mattress may have a few lumps and bumps, but before rushing out to buy a new one, ask yourself if this is the cause of your sleepless nights. If you're convinced your sleep could benefit from a better mattress, consider these factors:

- Health claims. Lolling in a billowy cloud of fluff—that is, a soft mattress—is out of date. It's firmness you're after—but don't be misled by extra-firm, ortho-firm, maxi-firm, or similar marketing labels. If the mattress—be it innerspring, foam, or inflatable—conforms to your body and still feels firm, consider it a possibility.
- Durability. Without sounding like an advertisement, you don't want to spend extravagantly for short-lived comfort. Durability is usually related to thickness, but look for details such as handles to turn the mattress, ventilation openings to help in air circulation, and plastic corner guards to protect the foundation.
- Safety. If insomnia and smoking in bed go hand in hand for you, recognize the risk: Mattresses are flammable.

The subject of beds is not complete without note of two rather unique structures:

- The electrically controlled, pushbutton bed. The home version of the electric hospital bed is particularly appropriate for people who find it difficult to turn over in bed, sit up, or lie down flat to go to sleep. In these instances, certain kinds of medical insurance coverage may help defray the comparatively high cost of such a bed.

- The water bed. These beds take up lots of space, require about two hundred gallons of water, weigh an enormous amount, and may develop leaks. If you have a friend who has one, try it before you buy it.

TEMPERATURE

Although the belief that cooler is better than warmer has not been proven, it seems to work for most people. An overheated bedroom can disturb your sleep throughout the night. Pre-warming your bed on cold nights (using an electric blanket if your electric utility rates seem reasonable) makes the sleep environment more inviting. An electric mattress pad, or even a hot water bag to your cold feet, does much the same thing. The hot water bag—unlike the electrical pad—has the additional safety virtue of not overheating if you should fall asleep on it.

ROOM LIGHTS

A lighted room keeps most people from falling asleep. Almost all of us have learned since infancy to live with a day-night rhythm. In this case, specifically, we go to sleep when there is darkness. Darkness becomes, then, both a time marker and a conditioned sleeping environment.

If you need to get up during the night, you might find a bedside flashlight, nightlight, or a dimmer light control useful. Some disposable flashlights have a small dime-size fluorescent spot that glows in the dark to help you find it. Nightlights are a bargain safety factor. If you or your bed partner likes to read in bed, try one of the newer bedside reading lamps. The narrow beam focuses only on the book page.

NOISE

On the one hand, noise can be what you make it. For example, a neighbor's barking dog may be either reassuring or annoying, depending on your experience with watchdogs or how meaningful that particular sound is to you. If neighborly diplomacy chills, you can then try to accept philosophically sound intrusion you cannot change, and consequently the noise might not trouble your sleep quite as much.

On the other hand, you might try making your bedroom more soundproof—such as using double windows, heavy drapes, or a thick carpet. You could try earplugs, a white noise machine, or even a radio playing softly.

It has been said that noise comes in two forms: the kind you hear and the kind that you don't hear. Experts say you do hear the kind you think you don't hear, such as passing cars or overhead aircraft, which cause a person already sleeping to shift into a lighter sleep stage. If you're a traveler, try to reserve a room with a quiet location. If your home is near a busy highway or airport, you might hang thermal-type drapes in your bedroom or use earplugs.

NIGHT CLOTHES

Bedclothes come in all sizes, shapes, and conditions. Marilyn Monroe is said to have remarked that all she wore to bed was Chanel No. 5. Be candid with yourself—if your longing for lacy French lingerie leaves you chilly, try an old-fashioned loose-fitting nightshirt. The idea is to be comfortable in bed.

HEARTBURN

A common affliction that can appear as you lie down to go to sleep, or even during sleep, may be heartburn—burning lower chest pain, sour taste, and coughing. The symptoms are a result of reflux of the acidic stomach contents back into the esophagus. Over time, and if not treated, the esophageal lining can be eroded by these uncomfortable episodes.

Among the simple practical steps you can take to relieve the symptoms are:

- Raise your upper body, either with pillows or by using blocks under the head of the bed. The goal is to prevent stomach acid from flowing back from the stomach into the esophagus.
- Don't wear tightly belted pajamas.
- Try antacid tablets, chewing them well, or use the liquid type antacid.

If symptoms persist, check with your doctor to make sure that a problem more serious than acid reflux is not present.

URGENT URGES

Awakening during the night to go to the bathroom is so commonplace, and can become so habitual, that this almost universal interruption of sleep may set the stage for an insomnia.

Not only may your level of wakefulness rise during a sleepy

barefoot trek on a cold floor or in a cold room, but overriding all the accumulated discomfort is the urgent demand by the bladder to empty itself forthwith and pronto. Sometimes the solution is as simple as cutting down on fluid intake in the evening, particularly stimulants such as tea, coffee, cocoa, and cola drinks. This is worth a try.

But chronic involuntary urinary spillage is a sleep disturbance of a different dimension. In men, leakage of small amounts of urine is a common disturbance, particularly during sleep. An enlarged prostate gland may be pressing on the urinary outflow structure, preventing complete emptying of the bladder. Only medical evaluation can determine which of many possible reasons is the cause of the involuntary leakage—called incontinence. Urinary incontinence in men and women is not the inevitable result of aging. With an accurate diagnosis, appropriate medical or surgical treatment can begin. Prompt nursing and medical care must go beyond minimizing discomfort to anticipate the prevention of complications, such as skin irritation due to urine.

Can an incontinent person be cared for at home?

Yes. Unless there are complications—such as bone fractures, stubborn infections, or mental confusion—many people can undertake the practical details of managing their urinary incontinence by themselves. For example, absorbent underclothing is available almost everywhere, and designed skillfully to avoid bulkiness. These underclothes are tailored to fit comfortably and many are disposable.

Exercise, usually taught by experienced nurse-educators or physiotherapists, can help strengthen bladder outlet muscles. Biofeedback training also may strengthen the muscles. If you learn how to control the urinary sphincter, you have the option of responding to a call from Mother Nature by returning the call later.

·4·

SLEEP FITNESS: PERSONAL SOLUTIONS FOR STRESS REDUCTION

Sleep fitness—how satisfied and refreshed you are by your sleep—reflects an old idea in a new light: that is, behavior is a language. The concept that your actions don't occur in a vacuum is a familiar and compelling piece of logic. Simply put, how you live during the day—how much daytime stress you are under—may affect how well you sleep at night.

The belief that the more relaxed you are, the more easily you will sleep is the guiding principle of this triple-focus sleep fitness program:

- One, taking inventory of how you live during your waking hours—a personal odyssey into self-awareness—and learning what can be changed to help you sleep.
- Two, learning "body-centered" relaxation methods.
- Three, learning "mind-centered" stress reduction skills.

SLEEP FITNESS CONNECTIONS

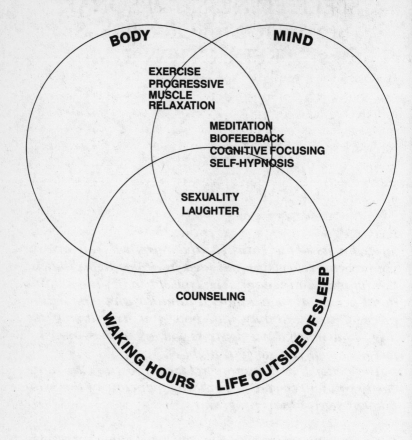

YOUR WAKING HOURS

I CAN'T SLEEP BECAUSE I CAN'T UNWIND AT NIGHT...

Look at what goes on for you during the day. Are you prone to a "hurry-up" syndrome—looking at your watch frequently, running for buses or trains, always short on time, eating fast, pushing yourself? Maybe you have one of those jobs where the work tempo is uncomfortably speeded up. Maybe you're one of those people who too often expect to sleep well regardless of what you do during the day. The daytime merry-go-round doesn't necessarily stop when you go to bed.

At first glance, it appears that the solution is being able to relax and turn off at bedtime. Although there are many relaxation techniques—and these are learnable—you have a sleeping problem that perhaps needs more remedy than learning how to relax only at bedtime.

HOW CAN I SLOW DOWN? WHERE DO I GO FROM HERE?

Start with the thought that perhaps your life style is interfering with your getting a good night's sleep. You will probably need to take a careful look at your pattern of living. If the pace of your life is too crowded, too rushed, you can, for example:

- Try to give yourself more time to do things. Take one step at a time.
- Sit down at breakfast time, eat more slowly, and chew each bite thoroughly before taking the next one.
- Allow more time to catch your bus, train, or carpool, if you're a commuter.

- Gain some welcome time in the morning by getting organized the night before—clothes, eyeglasses, cosmetics, commuter ticket, lunch box, wallet, briefcase papers, pillbox if you take midday medication.
- Unless you are on a medical program that requires stimulants, try to reduce those that you do take, such as caffeine, nicotine, or stimulant diet pills.

I'M ALREADY ORGANIZED TIME-WISE, AND I TRY TO TAKE ONE STEP AT A TIME. IT'S THE BIG THINGS THAT TROUBLE ME—UNPAID BILLS, AN AGING PARENT, TEENAGE CHILDREN, FAMILY CONFLICTS. . .

Even if you consider yourself the Rock of Gibraltar, you are not exempt from stress. No one is. Sometimes these anxieties are temporary, but often there is no foreseeable ending. Your attitude is just as important as the actual facts of a crisis or stressful situation, and can contribute to finding solutions. Trying to cope, to manage, or change these all too common and troublesome concerns can give you a sense of being in control. All you can do is the best you can do, and doing something may help you sleep better.

COUNSELING

Some problems of insomnia may be solved almost as simply as deciding to cut back on coffee, either on frequent daytime breaks or on the traditional after-dinner cup. However, when your problems are primarily rooted in suppressed feelings and attitudes, and when commonsense changes in your daily living don't improve your sleep, you may begin to feel over-whelmed.

Insomnia may be only one of the symptoms of your con-cerns, your sense of being anxious, or your feeling hopeless about the future. Even though you manage each day to keep in balance, you may be paying an invisible wear-and-tear price in additional symptoms, such as chronic irritability, anxiety, and impatience.

Talking out these problems with a sympathetic person will often help unbottle your feelings and clarify what can be done to change the situation. You might feel comfortable with a sensitive friend or a member of the clergy trained in pastoral counseling.

Pastoral Counseling

In many communities the individual to whom a troubled per-son first turns for advice is a member of the clergy. Men and women of religious commitment are concerned, very often, with the entire life of their congregation and do not limit themselves to matters of faith.

Most of the doctrinaire strife between science and religion is gone. Thousands of the clergy have taken postgraduate courses in pastoral counseling informing them what the pastor can do to bring living witness to the belief in human worth.

When consulted by someone burdened by longstanding problems, the experienced pastor sees this in the context of being helpful to the needy, not as a psychiatrist or psycholo-gist seeing a patient. No one expects a diagnosis from a pas-toral visit, but a member of the clergy—with some training and experience—can identify the size of the difficulty, refer you to a physician or health facility, and follow up the referral with ongoing concern. The sympathy and nonjudgmental understanding of such a trusted person may be the first crossroads you reach and may determine the direction treatment will take. The chronic anxiety underlying many insomnias can be so disruptive of both individual and family life that a knowledgeable pastor can literally turn the tide toward positive living.

Psychotherapy

You might, however, prefer counseling available from a trained professional psychotherapist. Practitioners of psychotherapy range among highly trained physicians and clinical psychologists, psychiatric social workers, nurse-clinicians, and family counselors. Professionals in these "helping professions" hold degrees from graduate schools, certificates based on passing state examinations, supervised clinical experience, and recognition of their authenticity by listings in specialized registries. Be certain that the person you consult is a qualified, licensed professional.

BODY-CENTERED RELAXATION SKILLS
EXERCISE

Mens sana in corpore sano—a sound mind in a sound body— is a truism that has been around since the days of the first century A.D. Despite its noble Roman origins, however, the search for a *"corpus sanus"* hasn't always been very fashionable. Indeed, a famous public leader once remarked that when the urge to exercise came upon him, he lay down until it went away.

Today you don't have to be an Olympic athlete to discover that the delights of a reasonable amount of exercise go far beyond a pleasantly attractive appearance. For starters, sleep may improve.

Exercise has found new therapeutic meaning in a workaday world that is increasingly sedentary, in a society that is daily and broadly stressed—nuclear threat, crime, office politics, social and family strife—and where a feeling of day-long exhaustion combined with nightly insomnia has become the listless handmaiden of an inactive, unconditioned body.

It is, however, annoying to be exhorted and prodded by sporty zealots to adopt an exercise program—particularly a daily, demandingly long regime of rigorous activity. As a newcomer, you probably wouldn't stick with it, for not only is unsupervised exertion dangerous, but trying to measure up to another's schedule can be discouraging. You know your own exercise boundaries. If you have any doubt about them, you'll be wise to check with your doctor.

You also know your own preferences. You don't have to jog. You can swim, bicycle, walk briskly, jump rope—all at your own time, place, and pace. For example, if a pool is nearby, and the roads in your neighborhood are too hilly for running, try swimming. Just a little bit, gradually, to get started. Almost everyone—even those with various medical conditions—can get into the swim with a gradual exercise medical prescription. Try to pick a time that doesn't interfere with your preparations for going to bed so you don't get too revved up to drift off to sleep.

You needn't feel achy, or breathless. You shouldn't feel pain at all. You will begin to feel well and totally fulfilled after your exercise. Eventually your physical repose will become a foundation for emotional tranquility and balance. Subtly, invisibly, you will find that you have acquired a skill that widens your capacity to absorb the knocks of the day and improves your chances at untroubled sleep.

PROGRESSIVE
MUSCLE RELAXATION

Progressive muscle relaxation has been around a long time. Many people may recall "phys ed" classes twenty-five years ago, when they fell asleep lying on the gym floor, the soothing voice of an instructor urging deep concentration on the toes. . . .

Progressive muscle relaxation is not exercise, like jogging or swimming. Like exercise, however, it is partly distraction therapy. The possible stresses of the office deadline, school exam, or overdue mortgage payment should slip into the background. Concentration, with eyes closed, lying down, clothes loosened, is basic to this skill.

Specifically, you will learn to focus attention on the muscle groups in your body where tension accumulates, such as the head and neck area. Alternatively tensing and relaxing these muscles, with practice and developing skill, can leave you feeling pleasantly at ease.

The tensing and relaxing teach you how to recognize what each muscle group feels like when it is really relaxed. This recognition is an important first step to learning "mind-centered" relaxation skills.

You might find it convenient to practice progressive muscle relaxation in groups, such as during office breaks or at health clubs after work. The skill, however, can be learned alone. Audio and video tapes are available to guide you through the steps.

DEEP BREATHING

Learning to fill your lungs with air and relaxing your abdomen can be part of progressive muscle relaxation exercises, or done by itself. Inhale slowly. When you exhale slowly, push all the air out of your lungs by contracting your stomach muscles slightly. Slowly saying to yourself "one one thousand" on inspiration and "two one thousand" on expiration gives a good measure of the pace.

Deep breathing for a few minutes before performing the following stress-reduction skills helps to ease you from the hustle-bustle of your busy day into the inner world of quiet you create for yourself.

MIND-CENTERED STRESS-REDUCTION SKILLS

STRESS REDUCTION SKILLS CAN BE LEARNED

Restoring a sense of balanced ease between mind and body has been the goal of philosophers and kings since ancient times. This, of course, is why the world has had so many enthusiastic promoters of pathways to that welcome calm whose trademark is untroubled sleep.

If, as the saying goes, practice makes perfect, you might try to encourage better sleep through stress reduction skills. The skills are learnable, have worked for many thousands of people, can help you reorder the many trains on your mind's tracks, and share the same premise—they quiet your mind and body without using drugs.

Something quite remarkable occurs as you acquire relaxation and stress-reduction skills. You not only create the opportunity to dispel your tension, but you may also develop the reserve to manage further stressful onslaughts.

At first you may feel that you have bitten off more than you can chew—but any skill worth its salt takes some time and effort to master. Once learned and used, stress-reduction skills have a lasting beneficial effect on overcoming troubled sleep as well as on other stresses in your life.

TRANSCENDENTAL MEDITATION

Transcendental meditation is a good place to get acquainted with some nondrug relaxation techniques. The popularity of TM has made it familiar almost everywhere.

The high-sounding phrase—transcendental meditation—belies the simplicity of this relaxation philosophy. TM is the pause that refreshes—or pauses, as people who use it practice twice or more during the day. Meditators repeat a special sound, called a mantra, silently to themselves. They allow this mantra to come and go, while comfortably seated, eyes closed, for about twenty minutes. In this way, the mind becomes uncluttered and an unthinking, soothing quiet follows. During this pause, your blood pressure can be lowered and your heart rate and breathing slowed down. The effect for many people is a sensation of diminished stress.

Not to be overlooked: TM does not depend on sedatives, tranquilizers, alcohol, or any other kind of drug. You can call your local or regional TM center for more information about learning the technique.

OTHER KINDS OF MEDITATION

There are many meditational techniques derived from all the cultures of the world. One of the most popular modern techniques was developed by an American doctor, Herbert Benson, who did the original physiological research on TM meditators. His meditation is called the "relaxation response."

According to Benson, you can bring about the same physiological responses as people do with TM by repeating a word like "one" to yourself, instead of a mantra. The important part of both techniques is to allow the word (or mantra) to slip easily out of your mind, if another thought appears. Then, when you notice it is gone, remind yourself to say it again, silently, to yourself. This alternation gradually teaches you to leave the other thoughts behind and expands the time during which the feeling of alert peace prevails.

For more information, adult education classes in your area may offer instruction in meditation techniques.

IS RELIGIOUS CONTEMPLATION OR PRAYER LIKE TM?

There are surface similarities between religious contemplation and TM, such as the withdrawal from activity and the focus on a silently repeated word. For many religious people, prayer or contemplation often ends the day peacefully. The medieval idea of a religious retreat as a pause in the onrushing world is still a living idea, not only for those of religious commitment but also for those who believe that periods of silence, withdrawal, and quiet soul-searching can restore equanimity.

The followers of TM maintain that their relaxation philosophy is not a religion. There are no sacred figures to worship in TM, and no reason to change any religious beliefs you already have.

ISN'T A SHORT NAP LIKE TM?

No. However, light sleep—the first of several deepening sleep stages—does resemble meditation. For example, oxygen consumption drops in both, but in TM it drops more quickly, indicating the body isn't working as hard. However lightly, you are *sleeping* when you take a nap. In transcendental meditation, you are awake in a kind of restful, but alert, quietude.

YOGA

Among the various belief systems to which people turn for a sense of tranquility is the Eastern doctrine called yoga. To an impatient Westerner, the concepts, practices, even vocabulary of yoga may at first make the achievement of an inner sense of peace seem remote. That inner peace can be a specific antidote to insomnia.

As with TM, yoga isn't a religion. The various doctrines of yoga are grouped around central ideas, such as the regulation of body postures, the ability to concentrate, the devotion to selfless service, and the repetition of a mantra, as in TM. Each daily activity is a sacrament.

Perhaps the most understandable brief description of the complexity of the various concepts of yoga is to call them attainment of complete mind and body mastery. If you have been suffering from chronic insomnia, one of the branches of yoga may offer the possibility of achieving a meditationlike ability to still the turbulence of the mind.

WHAT ABOUT BIOFEEDBACK AS A RELAXATION METHOD?

Biofeedback works—for patients motivated to learn. Biofeedback is based on the principle of self-regulation. You can control certain functions of your body that were long believed to be part of the involuntary nervous system, including, for example, blood pressure, gastric acid secretion, skin blushing, and heartbeat.

HOW DOES BIOFEEDBACK WORK?

Believe it or not, your state of mind, such as excitement or anxiety, can be expressed electrically. The link between the brain as a structure and the mind as its function is the electrical activity now called brain waves. For example, if you're angry or under pressure, your brain waves appear in a nonspecific pattern. If your feelings change, so does the electrical wave pattern.

This electrical activity can be displayed by a recording instrument. You can learn to recognize the changing signals, expressed by a tone or visually on an oscillograph. With practice, you can learn to put yourself into a state of mind corresponding to a particular signal.

The signals reflect brain-wave rhythms that are named, for example, alpha and beta. For purposes of relaxation, alpha rhythm is better than beta. With trial and error, and repeated attempts, most people find their way into alpha by thinking pleasant thoughts and recreating peaceful moods.

Biofeedback depends on brain-cell activity and on the ebb and flow of feelings. Your success in using it as a relaxation method depends on recognizing and capturing the moments of alpha rhythm.

WHERE IS BIOFEEDBACK AVAILABLE?

To learn how to use biofeedback, some people enroll in a training program with a specially trained psychologist. Often classes are held at university-based sleep centers. Or you can buy biofeedback devices and follow the instructions at home.

It is worth remembering that exploitation surfaces where there is a great need—such as a good night's sleep. Inflated prices and magical promises ride the bandwagon of this valuable twentieth-century discovery. So, try before you buy.

COGNITIVE FOCUSING

Sometimes the wish is father to the thought, and if those thoughts are rosy, so much the better. Cognitive focusing starts with this same premise: that if you can think positively about going to sleep, or going back to sleep after a middle-of-the-night awakening, you will have a better chance at untroubled slumber. With this in mind, you might try to:

• Think hopefully "I know I'll be back to sleep as soon as I let myself relax."
• Breathe slowly and deeply, in and out, ten times or more; start to focus on relaxing muscles from your toes to your head.
• Keep repeating calming thoughts to yourself.
• Continue to breathe deeply and focus on an easy and quiet mental image, such as a rose or your favorite beach.

This may sound too simple to work, but when practiced purposefully and regularly, cognitive focusing works better and better.

HOW IS SELF-HYPNOSIS DIFFERENT FROM MEDITATION?

Self-hypnosis and meditation are more alike than they are different. All the techniques previously mentioned can be thought of as a kind of self-hypnosis. They all use suggestion to selectively focus the mind—with a by-product of lessened anxiety.

You may be practicing self-hypnosis successfully right now without realizing it. By focusing your thoughts on an image or enjoyable memory, you may free yourself entirely from all distractions and attain a trance state of consciousness. This ability can be learned by almost anyone who is able to concentrate and has great motivation—for example, to overcome severe insomnia.

HOW IS SELF-HYPNOSIS DIFFERENT FROM HYPNOSIS DONE BY SOMEONE ELSE?

Some people find it too difficult to focus their minds using their own thoughts. For these people, the thought "go back to sleep" may be a much more powerful suggestion coming from a trained hypnotherapist than from inside your own mind.

You may be one of those people who is very susceptible to hypnotic suggestion. If so, the hypnotherapist can help you to accept sleep readily. A trance state is not sleep but its opposite: a wakeful, alert condition. In the highly receptive trance state, you can be told what to feel, what to do, and urged to do as you are told. You may be offered a particular word or idea to use yourself to initiate the trance at a later time, such as when you are ready for bed.

It's easy to confuse medical hypnosis with magician hocus-pocus. After all, vaudeville entertainers have misused it for years, and the practice still suffers from its association with quacks. If you consider, however, the many medical uses of hypnosis—dentists and physicians, particularly surgeons and anesthesiologists, practice it routinely—you can recognize that it can be an effective skill.

MORE ON SEXUALITY...

If both you and your partner find sexual expression fulfilling, sleep is a likely follow-up. But sex as a sleep aid can take on mythic proportions. After all, sexuality takes two to tango. When viewed simply as a sleep-inducer, sexual expression may leave overtones of insensitivity in your relationship. This therapy for the sleepless may be offensive to a partner who may not wish to become a human sleeping pill and because of its mechanistic posture. While the pleasures of sex may be thought of as skills and techniques, it is a comment on the casualness of human relationships to reduce such expression of intimacy to the status of a sleep aid.

As a sleep-inducer, sexual activity will show diminishing returns if you and your partner have a history of disappointing and conflict-ridden experiences together. A fundamental form of behavior between two people, sexual expression is prone to all the interpersonal tensions brought to any encounter—particularly if there are also sexual problems, such as impotence or anorgasmia. Frustrations of any kind, as well as powerful feelings such as anger, bitterness, or sadness may disturb sexual relations and may also disturb sleep. If your insomnia stems from this type of cause, you can probably benefit from some expert counseling.

All the same, with a creative and thoughtful attitude, sexuality may be considered among the arts of relaxation. If you and your partner feel a sexual responsibility toward each other, that the other's pleasure and gratification are yours as well, that all preferences are acceptable, your sexual expression may usher in a period of physical repose. When mutually satisfying sexual expression is such a comfortable, pleasurable, and relaxing feeling for you, you just might drift off to sleep.

LAUGHTER

Overcome by the fatiguing ravages of insomnia, you might find the idea of laughter as therapy a pretty sick joke at best and downright insensitive at worst. But the urge to laugh can be irrepressible. And, if actively pursued, laughter is drug-free, painless, and therapeutic.

If you are skeptical of the role of the chuckle, the broadening grin, the roaring guffaw, but if the feel of a good laugh appeals to you, you might be reassured by the successful experience of Norman Cousins, who wrote in *Anatomy of an Illness* (1979):

> Nothing is less funny than lying on your back with all the bones in your spine and joints hurting . . . a good place to begin . . . was with amusing movies . . . it worked. I made the joyous discovery that ten minutes of genuine belly laughter had an anesthetic effect and would give me at least two hours of pain-free sleep . . . the [intravenous] ascorbic acid was working. So was laughter . . . we stepped up the dosage . . . meanwhile the laughter routine was in full force. I was off drugs and sleeping pills. Sleep—blessed, natural sleep without pain—was becoming increasingly prolonged.

One laugh, however, does not a cure make. A "serious" laughter prescription should consider a well thought out program. You can include, as did Mr. Cousins, humorous movies, TV shows, cartoons, VCR replays, magazines, poetry—the list is limited only by your sense of humor.

The saying that laughter is good medicine underscores its actual systemic response. The umbrella of well-being engendered by laughter, according to Mr. Cousins: "creates a mood in which the other positive emotions can be put to work . . . creatively, the will to live, hope, faith and love have biochemical significance and contribute strongly to healing . . ."

HUGGING

The kind of open mind that can experiment with laughter as a mode of treatment is echoed pleasantly in some recent nursing care experiences. Pamela McCoy, R.N., a nurse-educator at Grant Hospital in Columbus, Ohio, was quoted in the "Lupus Foundation of America, Westchester Chapter, Newsletter" (October 1985): "We have found that people who are hugged or touched can often stop taking medication to get to sleep."

In agreement, Dr. David Bresler, of the Pain Control Unit at UCLA, was quoted in the same newsletter: "A hug can have an astonishing therapeutic effect by providing a sense of companionship and happiness."

This provocative idea is a resourceful option that no insomniac should overlook.

·5·

THE BIOLOGY OF TIME:
YOUR BIORHYTHMS

If you've been lying sleepless in bed every night until 2, 3, or 4 A.M., you may be a candidate for a biological rhythm tune-up. Don't be misled by the term "biorhythms": these are not avant-garde medicine, but reflect an ancient, basic guiding principle of life— rhythmicity.

You, the flora and fauna, day and night, are governed by a fundamental alternation that, like sleep and wakefulness and the seasons, forever cycle back and forth through existence.

Tides ebb and flow, plants open and shut their leaves, animals hibernate for the winter, day changes into night. Your temperature will edge up and down slightly over a twenty-four-hour period, through an invisible wax-and-wane cycle to include the basic rest-activity rhythm, dreaming, psychological performance indices, the systole and diastole of a beating heart.

Rhythmicity, like a celestial tick-tock, might be fascinating to explore in general, but specifically, your complaint of insomnia might be understood as an offbeat body rhythm whose sequencing and timing need to be adjusted.

I CAN'T MAKE MY 10 A.M. MORNING CLASS

If you have had a longstanding problem meeting morning commitments—such as school or work—you may be one of those people whose body rhythms are cycling on a schedule different from the nine-to-five workaday world you live in. This inconvenient, not to say tiresome, state of affairs can have a happy outcome. But first, does this not-too-common condition describe you?

- You lie in bed hours after retiring and rarely fall asleep before 2 A.M., and, often, not before 3 A.M.—although if you decide to turn in at 3 or 4 A.M., it usually takes only a few minutes for you to drift off.

- Once asleep, you sleep soundly and awaken refreshed if allowed to sleep through late morning or early afternoon— usually on weekends or vacations. Only with great effort will you arise earlier, and then with much irritability and prolonged sleepiness.

- You have had these going-to-sleep difficulties for months, and in many cases for years, occasionally beginning in childhood.

- You are a "night person," feeling most alert and productive in the late after-dark hours. Possibly, other members of your family show this same tendency.

- You have tried to treat your insomnia with pills, nightcaps, and olympic exercise. Nothing has worked.

GOING TO BED EARLIER DOESN'T HELP . . . CHRONOTHERAPY DOES!

Most "night people" who try to head off that next-day fatigue do not do well simply by going to bed earlier. On the other hand, a planned step-by-step delay in your going-to-bed time may work. As reported in *The New York Times* (May 22, 1979), Dr. Elliot Weitzman, an eminent sleep scientist, said that while "it seems to be relatively easy to reset a person's biological clock by moving it ahead, it is much more difficult to go in the other direction."

You may be instructed, for example, to go to bed three hours later each night. Working around the clock this way, in three-hour "steps," you eventually will arrive, within a week's time, at the hour you select to go to sleep. Not surprisingly, this "progressive" technique is called chronotherapy (*chronos* means "time" in Greek).

At home you may find that this measured shift in your going-to-bed time takes some doing. You will probably disrupt not only your daily routine but that of your family. Your sleep may also be uneasy. If need be, you can stretch your resetting program out six or seven weeks, allowing a week for each three-hour progression. Try not to give up or resort to a sleeping pill. It helps if you have a cooperative family or person with you.

If chronotherapy is carried out in the controlled environment of the sleep clinic, you can rely on your sleep therapist for guidance. After all, no man is an island.

JET LAG

Jet lag—when body time is Eastern standard and real time is Pacific coast—may inconvenience vacationers only transiently. But the jet lag fatigue, insomnia, diminished attention span, and possibly upset stomach may limit a businessperson's ability to make thoughtful, reasoned judgments. Indeed, many international companies make it a matter of policy not to schedule meetings on the day of arrival. A rule in the United States State Department mandates such advance time—often several days—to overcome the effects of jet lag. It's hard to be awake and functioning at peak performance when your body says "sleep."

Symptoms are due as much to not enough sleep as they are to disrupting your normal sleep-wake pattern. For example:

- You can't stay asleep long enough to feel refreshed.
- You're up and down all night.
- You tend to sleep at odd hours throughout the day and night.

"When in Rome do as the Romans do" makes good sense. Although it is impossible to reset your internal timing system instantaneously, there are methods around that claim to outwit the biological cycle, such as the Anti-Jet Lag Diet developed by Dr. Charles Ehret of the Argonne National Laboratory. For travelers staying more than a few days in a different time zone, Dr. Ehret advises a destination-time plan:

> . . . eating lightly the day before a long flight. The foods: eggs, cottage cheese, fish, salads, consomme, fruit—all low in calories and carbohydrates . . .
>
> The traveler should reset his or her watch—and behavior patterns—for destination time as soon as the plane is boarded.

Thus, if it is night where the traveler is headed, rest, rather than eating or watching the movie is in order. If it is daytime at the destination, the traveler should stay alert and keep active on the plane.

All meals should be eaten on destination time, especially a big, high-protein breakfast—even if that means bringing along the right food. On arrival, the traveler should eat big, high-protein breakfasts and lunches, and high-carbohydrate dinners for a day or two. And early to bed is the rule.

—*The New York Times,* November 28, 1982

To ease yourself into the new destination-time schedule, pay attention to the important time markers:

Activities—socialize and plan your day according to local time. Everything in moderation.

Meals—eat according to local time.

Light—get up and be outside as much as possible in the daylight hours.

YOU DON'T HAVE TO BE A JET SETTER TO HAVE JET LAG

Flying across time zones isn't the only way to temporarily disrupt your internal timing system. Today, particularly with the growing extent of twenty-four-hour industries and other all-night operations—such as the neighborhood supermarket—a wide range of people is exposed to the annoying and potentially dangerous effects of being out of sync with their environment.

Rotating shift workers may find ill-timed periods of sleepiness and poor reflexes uncomfortable. Long-distance truck drivers, police and firemen, air traffic controllers, and hospital staffs have a vital need to remain alert.

REGULAR HOURS AND ROTATING SHIFTS

While variety may be the spice of life in certain areas of behavior, regularity is the crucial, if not mundane, watchword for many basic activities. For example, going-to-sleep times. If you have a frequently changing or irregular sleep-wake schedule, you may be vulnerable to the unpleasant volley of disturbed body rhythms.

Unless shift workers can maintain their weekday schedules on the weekend too, they can throw their body rhythms—their internal timing systems—into turmoil. For example:

- The stomach will secrete acid at the usual mealtime, even though no food is present.
- A tired worker may chance pep pills or excessive caffeine to combat rising fatigue and further complicate his or her sleep-wake pattern with such stimulants.

If you can refrain from a mammoth sleep-in on weekends, vacations, and any off-work days and stick to the same going-to-bed and getting-up hours throughout, you won't play havoc with your biorhythms. And your sleep should be normal within a few weeks.

PRODUCTIVE SCHEDULING

If your life—work and otherwise—pivots uncomfortably on the hours you keep, chances are that your industry hasn't yet recognized the latest research in human biological rhythms.

Many companies rotate everyone in the work force through night shifts on a weekly basis. This is usually too short a time to settle in to a new body rhythm demand. Or shift hours are selected without thought to the highs and lows of individual biological rhythms.

If you are wearily trying to readjust all the time, you may be encouraged to learn that chronobiology—the study of the body's internal timing systems—is enlightening occupational medicine. On-site work studies have shown that sensitively planned rotations increase employee satisfaction and reduce employee turnover and the absentee rate for illness. At the same time, better-timed schedules increase productivity and strengthen the company's bottom line.

Most all-night businesses and industries have learned through experience that biological rhythms are a factor they must plan for. Designing the perfect twenty-four-hour schedule to fit everyone isn't easy. There is a spectrum of different variables that hedge the bet on setting up a single rotational system that suits each person. Consider these details:

- How much importance is accorded the effects of time shifts. Flight associations, for example, disagree over the severity of the disturbances experienced by pilots who are subject not only to time zone jet lag but also to the ups and downs of changing shifts.
- Other considerations include your age, the work you are doing, and, not least, your own individual biological rhythms.

While there may not be an overall rotation formula that works well for everyone, you can nonetheless campaign for a new design in your shift schedule. Any of the following might help:

- Longer times between shift changes. The rate of schedule rotation over the usual twenty-one- to twenty-eight-day shift is important to your ease in adjustment. At least ten days on each rotation appear to be the minimum time necessary to maintain health and job satisfaction.

- One to four days off between each shift change. This is a good time to anticipate new sleeping hours on the next rotation. You can begin a gradual change at this time.

- A later starting hour for each successive shift. The direction of your rotation—whether you change schedules by beginning at an earlier (phase advance) or later hour (phase delay) than you did on the last schedule—is also important to your adjustment. A phase-delay schedule is easier to adjust to, for the same reason your body adjusts more quickly to crossing time zones from east to west (phase delay) than from west to east (phase advance). The point is to move on your rotation in a clockwise way rather than counterclockwise (that is, move from days to evenings to nights rather than from days to nights to evenings.

In our current economic climate, preventive medicine and medical care benefits are vital issues in the workplace. Careful analysis of the effects of time changes may deliver higher productivity at lower cost, plus a no-expense lift in morale.

·6·

AGING: FROM MIDDLE
YEARS ONWARD

Statistics disclose that the landmarks of old age are being surpassed yearly. This medical evolution and social revolution are not exactly the fountain of youth, but nevertheless, you can anticipate a longer life.

The older troubled sleeper requires a special perspective. Metabolic systems have slowed; careers have changed, sometimes ended; and a sense of exclusion from life's enterprises is often a hazard of diminished exposure to stimulating experiences.

The possible consequences facing an aging population—lingering illness, loss of vigor—are conditions that, if understood and explored, can be treated so that you can enhance your vitality in the golden years. The tangle of many interacting medications you may be taking can be unraveled to give you easier nights; and the emptiness of a down mood can be dissolved to help overcome insomnia. It is more than possible to communicate again with life and to recover refreshing sleep.

I'M NOT SLEEPING AS MUCH AT NIGHT AS I USED TO. I'M GOING TO BED EARLY, BUT WAKING UP BEFORE DAWN. WHAT'S GOING ON?

The final act on how aging affects your sleep has not yet been written, but recent sleep research has come up with these important observations:

- You are probably sleeping the same number of hours you did when you were younger.
- The quality of your sleep—how "deep" it is—reflects the fact that more hours of sleep are spent in the lighter stages of sleep.
- The sleep-wake pattern (the basic rest-activity cycle)—so strong and defined between night and day in your younger years—appears to change with age. You may find yourself sleeping less at night and napping more during the day.
- Miniarousals of two to three seconds—normally, but only minimally, present in your twenties and thirties—are by age sixty significantly multiplied. You'll have no memory for these tiny waking punctuations of your sleep. They may, however, affect your feeling of alertness and energy the following day.

If you're feeling a bit weary from the seesaw of the subtle changes in the quality and pattern of your sleeping hours, consider these suggestions:

- Retire for sleep later rather than earlier. The early-to-bed/early-to-rise sleep-wake pattern can actually be a hazard to the sleep of the older sleeper. You may awaken too early in the morning (3 or 4 A.M.) and be tired later in the day, ready for nighttime sleep in the afternoon.

- Get up at the same time each morning.
- Try not to take multiple naps during the daytime.
- Remember that any of these gradual changes in your sleep may be only that—just changes. And may need a bit of getting used to.

ISN'T A NAP A GOOD IDEA IF I'M TIRED DURING THE DAY?

Yes, if you're the kind of person who can awaken from a nap feeling refreshed, and if you are willing to modify your sleep-wake patterns.

For example, a short daytime nap probably means delaying nighttime bedtime. Many people plan their days to include a nap. They flexibly satisfy sleep needs that are not met in the traditional nocturnal hours.

For some people, however, naps have become an escape from boredom or loneliness or the seeming formlessness of the day. You may awaken from such a siesta feeling irritable and still fatigued. A more stimulating and varied program of daytime activities might reduce this need for naps.

There are other ways to refresh yourself. Some of these may include relaxation techniques, exercise, or contemplative methods.

MEDICAL PROBLEMS AND INSOMNIA

A large number of medical conditions can disturb sleep. Pain from any source—for example, angina, arthritic joints, involuntary movement, abdominal distress, low back—can be severe enough to waken you or prevent you from sleep. The recurrent discomfort associated with reflux esophagitis ("heartburn"), asthma, aching legs, a stubborn cough, allergic rhinitis, or prostate enlargement with frequent middle-of-the-night trips to the bathroom can also trigger or prolong insomnia.

The sleep of people with a central nervous system illness, such as parkinsonism, is frequently altered by a change in the normal sleep-wakefulness patterns. Parkinsonian patients, for example, find that their sleep may occur in short napping-type episodes. The REM stage of sleep is so diminished in this disease that dreaming may spill over into the non-REM periods of sleep. Dreaming in this part of the sleep cycle can take the form of a night terror, punctuated by loud vocal outbursts and partial arousal. Adding to the troubled sleep of parkinsonism is the drug used to treat it—levodopa. Levodopa can cause spontaneous awakenings.

Sleep itself may sometimes aggravate an existing medical condition, particularly those illnesses that affect breathing and heart function. During the phases of slumber in which dreaming occurs, the body is enveloped in a cocoon of limp muscular flaccidity, but internally it is in a state of biological busyness:

- Peaks of biochemical and physiological activity correspond to variations in heart rate, respiration, and blood pressure.
- Certain enzyme levels rise.
- Genital excitation may occur.

People with a cardiac problem, for example, who are afraid of going to sleep because they fear a possible heart attack during the night, should discuss their concerns with a physician. He or she can determine whether the person is at risk or whether some of these natural worries are excessive.

It is tempting to hold the medical problem alone responsible for poor sleep. However, it comes as no surprise that where there is disease there is also a psychological response to it. For older people particularly, aging concerns—long-term illness, frailty, and dependency on others, as well as fear and anxiety over the ultimate outcome of a disease—can understandably contribute to sleeplessness, just as much as pain and physical discomfort do.

Frequently a person may be taking medication that can by itself cause difficulty sleeping. For example, ephedrine, a drug compounded for use as a nasal decongestant, is a powerful stimulant. The amphetamine appetite suppressants and steroid preparations may also cause severe insomnia.

When a medical problem and possibly medical treatment are contributing to your insomnia, you need the opportunity to describe these awakenings to your physician. Medication doses can be adjusted or the drug changed, or stopped. This adjustment needs to be monitored by your doctor, often step by step, and often with modifications due to changing body chemistry. With some knowledge on your part, some patience, and good communication between you and your doctor, you can multiply your chances for improvement.

MEDICATION HAZARDS

For the older person, medication may represent not only a treatment but a way of life. Yet consider these realities:

The Large Number of Pills

Drug prescriptions, over-the-counter sales, and borrowed medications are disproportionately high among older populations. Many older people are taking several medications—an average of six daily. As a result, keeping an orderly pill/dosage schedule throughout the day is a task easily open to interruptions and mistakes. So—check and double-check as you go along.

Repeat Prescriptions

Studies in Great Britain have disclosed the almost casual refilling of prescriptions for psychoactive drugs:

> Fourteen percent of all people aged 55 and over were taking psychotropic drugs (primarily sedatives and hypnotics) that had been prescribed more than a year previously. Nearly three-fifths of all repeat prescriptions for this class of drug had been obtained without seeing the prescribing physician . . . the older the individual, the longer she or he was likely to have a continuous prescription for psychotropics . . . with increasing age, the likelihood of seeing a physician when receiving the prescription was diminished.
>
> —Ruth Cooperstock, *Society and Medication: Conflicting Signals for Prescribers and Patients* (1983)

Slowed Metabolism

Your body no longer handles medications with the same efficiency and thoroughness it once did. If drugs cannot be metabolized or eliminated as promptly as they should, the medication can accumulate in your body in potentially harmful amounts. This is one of the major drawbacks of many sleep medications—the morning-after carry-over effects of grogginess and reduced alertness.

Certain groups of people at particular risk in using central nervous system depressant medication can be identified.

People Who Take Sleeping Pills and Alcohol

The person accustomed to an evening drink might decide to use sleep medication later that same night. The result is a confused, unsteady individual, unable to remember accurately just how many of what was taken. In this confused state, it is all too easy to take one more drink, one more pill, or both, seeking sleep but jeopardizing life. The wine of life should not be spilled so casually.

People Who Have Sleep Apnea and Take Sleeping Pills

Sleep apnea—a previously little recognized sleep disorder that is surprisingly common among elderly people—is a potentially life-threatening condition. It is impossible for sleep apnea sufferers to breathe while they are sleeping. They remain alive by hundreds of brief awakenings during which they breathe. The cycle includes heavy snoring, followed by a deep non-breathing silence, a sudden gasping for air, and then falling into sleep again. The many repetitions of this nighttime cycle are exhausting.

Daytime fatigue often follows, frequently accompanied by a feeling of depression and lessened sex drive. Because the disorder is relatively unfamiliar—and so rarely diagnosed—people already disabled by it may not recognize the additional dangers of using a sleeping pill for a "good night's sleep." The combination of a central nervous system depressant pill and breathing difficulty can be lethal. Discussion with your doctor is a *must*.

People Who Take Sleeping Pills and Other Medications

When the "other medications" are psychotropic drugs, such as sedatives, you run two risks:

- Possible toxic drug interactions, and
- Misdiagnosis of dementia. This is a particular hazard for elderly people. Memory impairment, decreased intellectual function, and slurred speech, for example, may represent organic brain disease, but may also be an overlooked drug reaction or a depression. Accurate diagnosis is crucial, and can mean the difference between managing an "incurable problem" and successfully reversing dementialike symptoms.

ARE OLDER PERSONS MORE PRONE TO DEPRESSION?

This is hard to answer with certainty. After all, older people may be reacting to a setting in which life's changes are around every bend. They may be facing the realities of serious illness, daily discomfort, possible poverty, social isolation, and borderline nutrition. The night can seem long and threatening. In the stillness of the dark, with few outside distractions, an older person may ruminate on the very fears and cares that keep him or her awake, heightening anxiety and vulnerability to depression.

It is important to recognize this type of depression early, if possible, to avoid years of misery or, indeed, prevent suicide. Sometimes serious depressions can be successfully treated by methods that include medication. As the depression lifts, sleep improves. So do other aspects of living, such as working, eating, social contacts, sexuality, energy—although readjustment of these long-time functions may take time and a supportive environment.

Some depressions—certainly not all—respond favorably to drug treatment. Good medical judgment can determine the important difference between a normal coping reaction to a passing life crisis and a major mood disturbance.

Pain/Depression/Insomnia

Insomnia is among the most distressing disturbances heightened by pain. Waiting in the wings, however, may be a significant complication: depression. Pain, depression, and insomnia form a troublesome triad that can become entrenched. Regardless of which condition came first, the impact of all three demands across-the-board intervention.

Because insomnia is one of the targets of your treatment, the role pain plays in charting your course needs clarification. Pain—and insomnia—have been all too often dismissed with the response "It's all in your mind." Of course it is. Where else would you expect to feel, understand, and cope with two of the most common human afflictions? For this reason, your pain problem is as uniquely specific as your fingerprints. This individuality alters your reaction to pain and can help or hinder you.

For example:

• If you're angry, frightened, or apprehensive, you intensify your pain and insomnia.
• If yours is a world where the stoic acceptance of pain without complaint—a stiff upper lip—is expected of you, you may be unaware that you are turning your back on effective treatment.

At the minimum, you can be reassured by the following facts:

- Helpful treatment to reduce your symptoms is almost always available. Therapeutic choices, such as precisely targeted pain-relief nerve blocks, have increased greatly in the past decade.
- Specialized pain units or pain clinic. The complexities of a longstanding pain problem—the medical, emotional, familial, occupational factors—make it very difficult for one doctor to take on seven-days-a-week responsibility for every aspect of your care. Pooling together the medical specialties—such as neurology, pharmacology, psychiatry, anesthesiology—means a wider network of expertise and more effective coordination of treatment programs is possible.

There is, without question, a host of judgments to be factored into the pain-relief jigsaw puzzle. Encyclopedic textbooks have been written about the pharmacology of analgesics (pain medication) and the various pain pathways in the body, and the physical processes of pain—to name only a few areas—and professionals have spent years developing experience, competence, and judgment in these matters.

If you feel reluctant to engage in such technical questions, consider that the real matter at issue is *you*. You have good reason to be informed about decisions made regarding your care.

Your determination to overcome pain and insomnia begins with accurate clinical information. Information, to be sure, is not an automatic cure-all. But it is a good start, especially if you begin with an uncomplicated guidebook, not a technically demanding textbook. In the next few pages, you can zero in on a few key areas.

PAINKILLERS

At one end of the spectrum of analgesic medications known as "painkillers" are the simple, "mild" compounds, such as aspirin, acetaminophen, or the nonsteroidal antiinflammatory drugs, such as ibuprofen (Motrin, for example). At the other end, there are the "strong" analgesics—the narcotics, with the pain-relieving capacity of morphine as the agreed-on yardstick for comparative analgesic studies.

Simple Analgesics, Nonnarcotic

Such drugs include: aspirin, acetaminophen (Datril, Liquiprin, Tylenol, Tempra); nonsteroidal antiinflammatory medications such as phenylbutazone (Butazolidin), indomethacin (Indocin), ibuprofen (Datril, Motrin, Nuprin)

It's been found that mild analgesics can diminish moderate, and in some cases, severe pain, and often eliminate the need for more potent medication. Simple analgesics usually are taken by mouth, and in therapeutic doses begin to act within forty-five minutes. Effects may last three to four hours. Tolerance and physical dependence do not develop.

Strong Analgesics, Narcotic

Such drugs include: morphine, heroin, codeine, oxycodone (Percodan), meperidine (Demerol), methadone, propoxyphene (Darvon)

The word narcotics conjures up visions of drug enforcement agents, the opium trade, smuggling, and derelict addicts lying in the gutter. The "street" aspect of narcotic drugs is very real, but when responsibly dispensed and rationally prescribed for relief of severe pain—carefully individualized for strength of dose, administration route (injection, tablet, elixir, solution, or suppository), and dosage schedule—narcotic analgesics are vital medical therapy.

When given round-the-clock to maintain an effective level in the bloodstream, narcotic analgesics can create a perception of less pain (you know the pain is still there, but it doesn't "bother" you) and less anxiety about pain recurrence.

These medications act on three fronts:

- relief of acute pain (for example, postoperative, or inoperative malignant illness, or severe trauma)
- elevation of mood (the euphoria experienced with some narcotics can lead to their abuse)
- inducement of sleep

ADDICTION

The relief of pain is the golden coin of twentieth-century medical science, but it is worthwhile remembering that the shining promise of one side must be balanced by the risks of misuse on the other. Whenever a substance can remove a sense of pain, disordered sleep, or melancholia and replace these conditions with a sense of well-being and restorative sleep, that substance has the potential for abuse (alcohol is the leading candidate).

The fear of addiction to narcotics used for pain relief trembles on the verge of myth:

- The myth: Narcotics are always addicting, no matter how they're used.
- The reality: Whereas certain people—for example, those who abuse alcohol or other drugs—may be susceptible to the addictive potential of a narcotic medication used for pain relief, surveys of the general population suggest that

long-term medical use of narcotics does not automatically lead to addiction.

- Another myth: "One shot and you're hooked."
- The reality: People differ widely in terms of the time taken for tolerance (the need to increase the dose to maintain the original effect) to occur and dependency to begin.

Narcotic addiction in the pain-relief setting needs some clarification:

- Over time, with long-term use (for example, multiple daily doses for at least twenty days), tolerance can develop, although individual response to this varies.
- Over time, withdrawal symptoms—for example, insomnia, fever, tremors—can develop on abruptly stopping narcotic medication, evidence of physical dependency, not addiction.
- Physical dependency and tolerance—in the pain-relief setting—can be modified by your doctor. This can occur by changing the delivery of your medication from injection to a form you swallow, slowing the absorption of the drug, switching from one narcotic drug to another, or withdrawing in a slow, step-by-step plan.
- Physical dependency and tolerance are not addiction, which is a kind of bondage to, or craving for, the drug over and beyond its use for pain relief.
- Narcotics used medically for analgesia and those abused on the street may be the same drugs, but the patterns of use, the psychosocial circumstances in which they are taken, are entirely different.
- Research suggests that medical use of narcotics is rarely associated with addiction.

Doctors and nurses who have seen the miseries of addiction may "underdose" pain-relieving medications to avoid this risk. Pain relief has enough yes/no precautions without adding inadequate dosage of medication to the list. In *Pain: Mechanisms and Management* (1982), Kathleen Foley, M.D., Director of the Pain Clinic, Memorial-Sloan Kettering Cancer Center, New York, wrote "There is no therapeutic regimen more dependent upon the prejudice of the individual prescribing physician than the use of narcotic analgesics."

Contributing to the medical community's general reluctance to use narcotic analgesics clinically are:

Fear of Addiction and Drug Dependency

The truth of the matter, as just stated, is worth repeating: Rational medical use of narcotic analgesics is rarely addicting. Experience in hospices, for example, has shown no need for increased doses of narcotics prescribed over a period of months. Pain relief is a legitimate, time-honored goal of medicine. In the face of the often unnecessary suffering of chronic pain, the popular image of a seedy, desperate addict, seeking drugs, is simply irrelevant. Most patients in medical care settings who have been taking large doses for a considerable time are able to stop even such potent drugs as morphine.

Crossed Signals

Sometimes your physician isn't aware of crucial bits of your pharmacological particulars, such as:

when the drug begins to take effect for you

when it begins to wear off

whether you have any side effects from the drug

Your feedback increases the likelihood of choosing the most beneficial medication, in the appropriate strength and dosage schedule.

Uncertainty Over the Diagnosis

Doctors are hesitant to prescribe in the absence of a proven diagnosis. Detailed diagnostic studies often take time.

Multiple Medications

If you are taking two or more medications—for example, for high blood pressure, emphysema, arthritis, water retention, or kidney function—your doctor must consider the intricacies of their biochemical interactions when introducing a new drug or dosage schedule.

Side Effects

Your doctor may be concerned with side effects, such as excessive sedation, constipation, nausea, and vomiting. The possibility that this will happen varies from patient to patient.

SEDATIVE/TRANQUILIZER

Sedatives create a diminished awareness of the environment. Strictly speaking, they are not primarily painkillers, but in reducing anxiety, sedatives can lessen your sense of pain, allay your worry about pain recurrence, and thereby encourage sleep.

Consider, however, the implications of having a "diminished awareness." When the President of the United States was admitted to the Bethesda Naval Hospital as a surgical patient, an intricate network of governmental authority was arranged to anticipate any contingency. One of the most serious of those contingencies is the possibility that the President may be unable to carry out his responsibilities, especially when surgical procedures require preoperative medication, surgical anesthesia, the relief of postoperative pain, and the restoration of sleep.

If the press and TV media carry the government's report that the president is sedated, on this word pivots the minute-to-minute transfer of power of the presidential succession. With such use of sedation, here are some questions that surface:

- How long will he be sedated?
- Is he transferring his powers to the vice-president? (Can any national leader be asked to keep an ever-alert finger on the nuclear button while having a "diminished awareness" of what's happening?)
- Is the president capable of judging these questions while undergoing treatment?
- Will postoperative pain medication call into question his ability to retrieve his elected authority? (The vital issue of his disability is for the president to resolve or dismiss. The Constitution implies that if the president says he's capable to discharge his duties, he's capable.)

Note that the medical bulletins about the president did not say he was drowsy, lethargic, soporific, stuporous, tranquilized, comatose, or unconscious—all states of mind having different places along the spectrum of global awareness. A unique place in this historical moment was occupied by the word "sedated."

The use of the word "sedative" in a coined word combination—as in hypnotic/sedative—is now accepted by the medical community to mean:

- A hypnotic drug sedates—but does not induce sleep—when given in divided doses during the day.

- The same drug will induce sleep when given in a large dose at night.

ANTIDEPRESSANTS

Such drugs include: Tricyclics, such as amitriptyline (Elavil, Endep, Tofranil, Vivactil)

Quite apart from their use to elevate mood, the tricyclic antidepressants have often been effective in the treatment of pain, particularly for neuralgias and chronic pain syndromes. As a result, with the use of tricyclics, sleep may improve. Research suggests that the tricyclic antidepressants can be useful for the pain-depression-insomnia triad.

ANALGESICS OR ANALGESIA?

At this point, it seems worthwhile to comment on the tendency to consider pain relief as only pills, injections, and other substances. It is all too true that many people turn to taking "something" to relieve emotional pain and the common but transient miseries of the human experience—an often unsatisfactory way to bypass the "tincture of time" response. This pill mind-set is subtle. The concept of quick relief and easy answers to stressful events in your life may lure you to regard analgesics in the same simplistic way.

Analgesics—the pharmacopeia of injections, elixirs, pills, suppositories—are not the "be-all and end-all" of pain relief. Many times they are not "at all" the answer, particularly if yours is a long-term condition for which the risks of dependency may weigh too heavily, or if no specific cause can be found for your pain.

Analgesia—a word with Greek roots—means the abolition of pain. From this more wide-reaching point of view, there are promising and proven alternatives that range from injected pain-relief nerve blocks, physical therapies, to psychological strategies, biofeedback, meditation, medical hypnosis. You may prefer and welcome these nondrug regimens:

Electrical Nerve Stimulation

The application of a battery-powered pulse generator to the skin may provide hours of pain relief with as little as five to thirty minutes of usage. Such nerve stimulation has been effective in easing neck and low-back pain in particular, as well as in relieving amputation stump pain and postherpetic neuralgia.

Biofeedback

As a pain-relief therapy, biofeedback has been most useful with relaxation of muscle tension. Neck pain and muscle-tension headaches have responded successfully to this technique.

Medical Hypnosis

Hypnotherapy, as a form of psychotherapy, may reduce anxiety through concentrated suggestion. The method has been used effectively—singly and in combination with other treatments—in many pain states, such as burns, migraine headache, and cancer pain.

PAIN RELIEF

Frequently Used Analgesic Medications

SIMPLE ANALGESICS, NONNARCOTIC

Includes: Acetylsalicylic acid (aspirin)

Acetaminophen (Datril, Liquiprin, Tempra, Tylenol)

Phenylbutazone (Butazolidin)

Indomethacin (Indocin)

Ibuprofen (Advil, Motrin, Nuprin)

NARCOTIC ANALGESICS

Includes: Morphine

Heroin

Codeine

Oxycodone (Percodan)

Meperidine (Demerol)

Methadone

Propoxyphene (Darvon)

Hydromorphone (Dilaudid)

OTHER MEDICATIONS USED IN ANALGESIC SETTING

Includes: Diazepam (Valium)

Amitriptyline (Elavil, Endep)

Nondrug Therapy Alternatives

Includes: Biofeedback

Medical hypnosis

Psychological methods

Physical therapy

Acupuncture

Contemplative practices

Electrical nerve stimulation

Regional nerve block

· 7 ·

DISORDERED SLEEP: NARCOLEPSY AND SLEEP APNEA

It may seem ironic to speak of insomnia—too little sleep—and too much sleep in the same breath. How can one exist with the other, its apparent opposite? The insomnia that is experienced as not getting enough nighttime sleep is also a feature of a distressing condition of too much sleep.

Overwhelming daytime sleepiness may be part of a constellation of primary disorders of the brain's sleep-wake mechanism. Such unnatural sleepiness is a neurological illness that has profound repercussions on the lives of patients and their families. An accurate diagnosis and professional treatment can bring relief and a measure of control to those afflicted by both excessive daytime sleepiness and nighttime insomnia.

NARCOLEPSY . . . TOO MUCH SLEEP?

Narcolepsy, a not-so-rare, genetically transmittable sleep disorder, has been loosely named "sleeping sickness." Indeed, it is an illness of excessive daytime sleepiness. Yet this is not sleep as you normally experience it, but rather a cruel distortion of it because there is a breakdown in the timing and boundaries between sleep and wakefulness, particularly between dreaming and wakefulness. The results of this breakdown for a narcoleptic include:

- The day is broken up by a series of brief and repetitive sleep attacks. The victim is unable to resist sleeping on the job, for example. He or she may doze off during a meal, or in conversation, standing up, or sitting down, or even while driving a car. Despite the periods of sleep, the pervasive background is unremitting lethargy.
- The general lack of muscular movement, ordinarily found in normal dreaming sleep, occurs briefly and suddenly during wakefulness. Often these episodes—known as cataplexy—are triggered by such enjoyable feelings as laughter and excitement, during which the person crumples into a heap.
- A similar feeling of inability to move may occur at specific times, such as going to sleep or on waking up.
- Normal sleep does not begin—as narcolepsy does—with a period of dreaming. Dreaming generally occurs after approximately the first ninety minutes. Narcoleptics not only begin their sleeping episodes with vivid dreams, but they are likely to experience these while still somewhat awake. These hypnogogic hallucinations, as they are called, are dreams that intrude into the waking state.

The nighttime sleep of narcoleptics is often troubled. Insomnia may command only passing attention with a presenting complaint of too much daytime sleep, but sleeplessness at night is common, with restlessness, frequent awakenings, and nightmares.

The restorative benefits of normal nighttime sleep or even of a catnap are not forthcoming. Sleep, on a background of constant drowsiness, is unrefreshing.

The personal lives of patients and their families are witness to the crippling effects of narcolepsy—loss of work, broken marriages, social isolation, depression.

CONTROLLING NARCOLEPSY

Sensitive and adroit medical monitoring can offer the narcolepsy sufferer a measure of satisfactory daily living. That measure can take several forms:

- Self-searching in counseling sessions to express the "down" feelings a chronic illness brings.
- Scheduling short, strategically timed naps during those daytime periods when sleep attacks are apt to occur, such as lunch hours or after meals.
- Informing friends, family, and acquaintances about your illness and about how you plan to live as normally as possible.
- Controlling sleep attacks and cataplexy with carefully chosen medication. Stimulant drugs can increase alertness and are effective in cutting down the number of sleep attacks from perhaps several per day to several per month. Tricyclic antidepressant drugs can significantly reduce the episodes of cataplexy. Tolerance, dependency, and side effects such as irritability, sexual problems, and obesity are common enough, however, to warrant drug holidays.

SLEEP APNEA . . . TOO LITTLE SLEEP?

"As I live and breathe" is one of those old-fashioned pithy exclamations that packs much meaning into a few words. The many-sided connection between insomnia and the breath of life is seen most readily in a group of several related sleep disorders called sleep apnea—"apnea" being based on Greek words that translate as "no breath." People with sleep apnea can live and breathe as long as they're awake, but it's impossible for them to sleep and breathe at the same time.

A stop-and-go repetitive pattern—in which respiration is impossible during sleep and continuous sleep impossible during breathing—alternates nonbreathing sleep periods with many brief breathing awake periods. The cycle, punctuated by heavy snoring, a feeling of suffocation, choking, and gasps for air, is exhausting.

Differences among the various "no breath" disorders are important diagnostic signposts. Successful treatment—medical or surgical—depends on pinpointing which type of sleep apnea is being confronted: obstructive or central.

Obstructive Apnea

During sleep, an obstruction, such as grossly enlarged tonsils, an enlarged tongue, or excess fatty tissue in the throat, blocks the airway.

Central Apnea

Without the normal regularity of coordinated central nervous system impulses, the chest and diaphragmatic muscles do not exert their usual synchronized inhale-exhale bellows effect on respiration.

SNORING, CHARLES DICKENS, AND THE PICKWICKIAN SYNDROME

While lethargic fat Joe who snored loudly is an invention of Charles Dickens in the *Pickwick Papers,* the spinoff—the pickwickian syndrome—is in public domain. The syndrome is no longer regarded as droll humor but a potentially lethal condition. The constellation of symptoms this syndrome represents is often a feature of sleep apnea:

Obesity

Obesity is commonly seen among sleep apnea sufferers, and often interferes with normal breathing and cardiac function. Weight loss can dramatically improve the ability to breathe, reduce the degree of heart failure, and increase a sense of well-being.

Snoring

Loud snoring may be a sign of nothing more serious than a stuffy nose. On the other hand, snoring may be the clue to a sleep apnea: All apneics snore constantly, often thunderously. Bedroom partners are not only awakened by the snoring, but they are also frequently forced to find another room for quiet sleep.

Daytime Lethargy and Sleepiness

The many nonbreathing nighttime episodes create a periodically inadequate body oxygen level so that daytime function also is eroded. Dulled reflexes and diminished alertness can lead to accidents, frequent nodding off, and, as in narcolepsy, inability to carry on activities of daily living.

Medical Complications

The irregular on-off breathing pattern places extra demands on the heart and blood vessels. After a period of time, high blood pressure, cardiac arrhythmias, and possible stroke can occur.

SLEEPING PILLS, NIGHTCAPS, AND SLEEP APNEA

You might be surprised to learn that sleep apnea has been found in a substantial number of "normal" elderly adults—unbeknown to them. When a fully developed sleep apnea can exist without your knowing it, you can possibly be the unintentional victim of your own lack of information. Feeling out of sorts and tired from a restless night and repeated awakenings, you may understandably take what seems to you to be a sensible and harmless step toward relieving your insomnia: sleeping pills.

The unwitting taking of sleep medication or an occasional nightcap—even a social drink—is one of the hidden hazards of sleep apnea. Here is why:

- Many people are in the dark about the life-threatening effects of central nervous system depressant substances on a breathing problem, such as sleep apnea. The combination of nonbreathing periods and central nervous system depressant medication—sleeping pills, tranquilizers, sedatives, alcohol, barbiturates—seriously reduces vital functions, such as respiration.
- Many people also don't know they have sleep apnea.
- The largest segment of society using prescribed sleep medication, and other medications, is over age sixty. This is the same population in which sleep-disordered breathing is most common and in which sleep apnea often goes unrecognized and undiagnosed.

CONTROLLING SLEEP APNEA

An oft-repeated saying is that half the solution is recognizing the problem. If left unrecognized, or untreated, the specter of constant sleepiness so common in sleep apnea can severely handicap the marital, financial, and social fabric of life. The seeds of such medical complications as obesity, high blood pressure, or cardiac arrhythmias may take root and become a dangerous threat.

Successfully controlling sleep apnea means beginning with an important step: recognizing the problem. This may be easier said than done. You may be untroubled by daytime sleepiness and be unaware of nighttime apnea. The nonbreathing episodes are occurring, after all, when you're asleep. Your bedroom partner is often the first to urge you to bring your dramatic nighttime symptoms—the not-so-comic snoring and gasping for air—to the attention of your doctor. Spouses sometimes bring the doctor a valuable report—a tape recording of the cycle of difficult respiration.

You may be tempted to go it alone, trying naps if you're sleepy during the day or taking a nighttime sleeping pill if you're unrefreshed by your fitful dozing. This is an area, however, in which medical attention is essential. To precisely determine whether a person's problem is due to an airway blockage or to scrambled messages from the brain centers controlling breathing is a demanding medical challenge. A thoughtful treatment plan and carefully selected medication are vital to improve quality of life at the very least.

At the most, they are literally lifesaving.

As symptoms are differently expressed in each case, treatment can take several forms:

Weight Loss

For some, especially when sleep apnea is associated with obesity, treatment may consist entirely of a weight-reduction program. Generally, reducing obesity, if it is present, is the first stage in treatment after a diagnosis is made.

Medication

Several drugs have been used in the hope of lessening the symptoms of sleep apnea. As this is a complex, evolving field in clinical pharmacology, your doctor is the best guide to the latest information.

Changing Sleep Position

Sleeping on your back may increase the number of non-breathing episodes because of airway obstruction. Try to sleep on your side.

Treatment of Medical Complications

Irregular heart beat, congestive heart failure, and high blood pressure may be noted and can be concurrently treated. Depression is a frequent complication in prolonged illness. Antidepressant medication and mental health counseling may be recommended.

Continuous Positive Airway Pressure (CPAP)

Mechanical ventilators—respirators to assist breathing—are familiar equipment in hospitals and clinics. A home-size unit has recently been developed to help prevent sleep apnea. The device, called CPAP (continuous positive airway pressure), consists of a mask that fits over the nose. The mask is attached to a hose and air-pumping unit. A continuous stream of air averts collapse of the throat and airway. Used at night, CPAP may alleviate nighttime snoring and daytime tiredness. Wearing the mask may be a nuisance at first, or mouth-breathing may be troublesome for you, but most people become motivated to continue using CPAP when they notice the difference it makes in their lives.

Surgery

In general, surgery is not a first step in the treatment of obstructive sleep apnea. When elected, surgery can repair specific obstructive conditions, such as blockages in the nose or throat (including enlarged tonsils and adenoids) or a deviated nasal septum. Surgery to enlarge the airway space may significantly reverse symptoms, but should be considered only if:

- The daytime sleepiness is so disabling that your daily activities and quality of life are compromised.
- Life-threatening irregular heartbeat occurs.
- Other medical treatment has not improved the condition.

·p·a·r·t· t·w·o

A READER'S GUIDE

·8·

A VISIT TO A
SLEEP LABORATORY

If you have been referred to a sleep-wake disorders center or clinic, you will find this information useful in helping you to get the most out of your visit. You may have traveled a frustrating and weary path to this point. Probably your insomnia has been a long-term problem—thwarting at least one month's efforts to treat it.

The sleep lab beckons at the forefront of technology, but you would be wise to look before you leap. Sleep experts have questioned the overall contribution of the sleep laboratory evaluation in the treatment plan for insomnia. Also, the clinic experience may be expensive and time-consuming, and you may encounter costly travel expenses. Most centers, usually located in metropolitan areas, are often at some distance from the total geographic population served.

The clinic team and elaborate equipment of a sleep-wake clinic are basically diagnostic. Rarely do they engage in long-term patient care. You will be expected to have a referring doctor, if one is available, in your own community—someone who can interpret the sleep center diagnosis, monitor any medications, and fit the treatment plan to your overall medical status and pattern of living.

A little-known function of some sleep laboratories is the investigation of the causes of male impotence—anatomical, endocrine, or psychological. The link between this disturbing problem and the sleep laboratory is not so obvious at first. The fact, however, that erections normally occur—in males of every age group, from infants to eighty- and ninety-year-olds— several times nightly during specific stages of sleep means that observations can be carried out using polysomnographic techniques. The NPT (nocturnal penile tumescence) study can be done when a thorough medical and psychological examination has indicated that more information is needed to precisely determine the cause, or causes, of impotence.

Be prepared, however, for a lengthy visit. An evaluation can typically take several days and nights. In addition to the usual measurements taken in a sleep laboratory—for example, the electrocardiogram and electroencephalogram—erections are measured using an elastic cuff around the penis.

Among the professional staff at a sleep-wake disorders center are neurologists, psychiatrists, and clinical psychologists. In addition, specialists in every field of medicine and surgery are available. There are people trained in electronics and engineering to operate the technical equipment.

Your doctor will be asked to provide your medical record, including, if available, copies of pertinent medical lab tests, electrocardiogram (ECG), electroencephalogram (EEG), and x-rays, as well as neurologic and psychiatric reports. At its most elaborate, a sleep center evaluation will include:

- a complete medical and sleep history
- physical examination (general and neurological)
- assessment of home sleep diaries, if available
- screening psychological interview and tests
- your monitored sleep at the lab
- discussion and review by the staff

A VISIT TO A SLEEP LABORATORY

Probably, before your visit to the sleep laboratory, you will receive some advance preparation in the form of a kit, including information on:

- Fee schedule (initial consultation, follow-up visit with staff physician, nap and/or overnight sleep lab tests)
- A medical record release to be given to your medical doctor
- When to arrive and where
- What to bring (pajamas, toothbrush, essential medications, reading material)
- Description of a medical center sleep laboratory. Much of the laboratory often consists of several small private rooms, sometimes called "time isolation units" because of the absence of environmental cues, such as clocks or windows. There are bathroom and shower facilities. Each room includes video and audio monitoring equipment.
- Polysomnography. The syllables of this imposing word explain its meaning—many sleep recordings. The term refers to the collective electrographic recordings of a variety of body activities. The measurements are painless and can record:

Sleep stages (the electrode leads—small coin-size patches that stick onto the skin Band-Aid fashion, or with paste—are usually attached to the scalp, sides of the face, and under the chin)

Eye movements

Heartbeat (electrocardiographic leads)

Leg movements

Breathing

Body temperature

Blood oxygen (a warmed earpiece shines light through a part of the ear to determine blood oxygen content)

Penile erection (can help determine whether male impotence is anatomical or psychological, or both)

- Sleep lab technicians. The sleep lab technicians may use a paste—somewhat like toothpaste—to attach the electrode leads to you. Throughout your testing a technician will remain in a room next to yours to monitor the recordings and be available for assistance.

A week or two after you have completed your sleep laboratory studies, you will probably have an appointment with your doctor or the sleep center doctor to discuss the findings. Specific medical, pharmacological, and psychological recommendations may be in order. Don't be disappointed if the doctor has no simple or quick pill or prescription to offer to you. You may be advised to try treatment alternatives that have an effective and successful track record—psychotherapy, behavior modification, relaxation skills, exercise, and contemplation.

·9·
OFTEN USED (AND ABUSED) SLEEP MEDICATIONS

This section is an abbreviated reference source for practical information and comparison among some of the most widely used medications and substances taken to bring on sleep. The following profiles represent not a compendium of all hypnotic products, but a useful and quickly accessible baker's dozen.

DIAZEPAM

Brand Name	Valium (Roche), U.S.A.
	Valrelease (Roche), U.S.A.
	Valcaps (Roche), U.S.A.
Chemical class	Benzodiazepine
Street name	Vals, blues, downers
Prescription required?	Yes
Available in generic form?	Yes

Intended use	Relief of mild anxiety, transient situational stress, localized skeletal muscle spasm, symptoms of alcohol withdrawal, and seizure disorders. Not for use in children under six months.
Dosage form	Tablets; timed-release capsules; injection
Dosage strength	Depends on intended use. Scored tablets: 2 mg, 5 mg, 10 mg; timed-release capsules: 15 mg
Withdrawal symptoms?	Yes, often after stopping medication abruptly. May include insomnia, seizures, muscle cramps, vomiting, tremor, weakness, and depression.
Side effects	Central nervous system slowdown; includes degrees of residual daytime drowsiness.
Undesirable effects	May involve several body systems, particularly the central nervous system—causing, for example, dizziness, staggering, headache, irritability, weakness, slurred speech, sweating, urinary incontinence, constipation.
Overdosage effects	Severe central nervous system depression, ranging from lethargy to comatose states; diminished reflexes.
Length of action	Long-acting; half-life of 27–37 hours
Precautions *Drug interactions*	Possibly lethal if alcohol, tranquilizers, antihistamines, seizure medications, or other central nervous system drugs have been taken.

Precautions

Drug interactions (continued)	Cimetidine (Tagamet), taken as peptic ulcer medication, may prolong effects of diazepam.
	Contraceptive pills significantly prolong effect of diazepam.
Special at-risk persons	Those over age sixty and persons with severe liver disorders have increased susceptibility to daytime hangover reactions and side effects.
	Pregnant and/or nursing women: avoid use.
Habit forming?	Dependency likely, except for short-term or intermittent use.
Noteworthy	Approved for more uses than any other benzodiazepine drug. Usage of this drug disqualifies user for aircraft piloting. Drug effects in the elderly may be mistaken for senility or dementia, leading possibly to inappropriate treatment.

FLURAZEPAM HYROCHLORIDE

Brand name	Dalmane (Roche), U.S.A. Dalmane (Roche), Canada
Chemical class	Benzodiazepine
Street name	None
Prescription required?	Yes
Available in generic form?	No

Intended use	To promote sleep
Dosage form	Capsules
Dosage strength	15 mg, 30 mg Not recommended under 15 years
Withdrawal symptoms?	Yes, often after stopping medication abruptly.
Side effects	Central nervous system slowdown; includes degrees of residual daytime drowsiness.
Undesirable effects	May involve several body systems, particularly central nervous system—causing, for example, dizziness, staggering, headache, irritability, weakness, slurred speech, sweating.
Overdosage effects	Severe central nervous system depression, ranging from lethargy to comatose states; diminished reflexes.
Length of action	Long-acting; half-life of 74–160 hours
Precautions *Drug interactions*	Possibly lethal if alcohol, tranquilizers, antihistamines, or other central nervous system drugs have been taken. Cimetidine (Tagamet), taken as peptic ulcer medication, may prolong effects of flurazepam.
Special at-risk persons	Those over age sixty have an increased susceptibility to daytime hangover reactions and side effects. Pregnant and/or nursing women; persons with depression.

Special at-risk persons (continued)	Some types of glaucoma may be worsened.
Habit forming?	Dependency likely, except for short-term or intermittent use.
Noteworthy	Usage of this drug disqualifies user for aircraft piloting. Drug effects in the elderly may be mistaken for senility or dementia, possibly leading to inappropriate treatment.

LORAZEPAM

Brand name	Ativan (Wyeth), U.S.A., U.K.
Chemical class	Benzodiazepine
Street name	None
Prescription required?	Yes
Available in generic form?	No
Intended use	Relief of anxiety and insomnia due to anxiety; preanesthetic.
	Not for use in children under age twelve.
Dosage form	Scored tablets; 0.5 mg, 1.0 mg, 2 mg., injection
Dosage strength	Depends on intended use.
	Reduced dose for elderly or frail persons.

Withdrawal symptoms?	Yes, often after stopping medication abruptly. May include insomnia, seizures, muscle cramps, vomiting, tremors.
Side effects	Central nervous system slowdown.
Undesirable effects	Sedation, dizziness, weakness, staggering
Overdosage effects	Severe central nervous system depression, ranging from confusion, somnolence, to coma.
Length of action	Short-acting; half-life of 8–25 hours
Precautions	
Drug interactions	Do not take with alcohol or other central nervous system depressants.
Special at-risk persons	Cautious use in elderly patients and in those with impaired renal function.
	Pregnant and nursing women: avoid use.
	Some types of glaucoma may be worsened.
Habit-forming?	Yes, except for short-term or intermittent use.

TEMAZEPAM

Brand name	Restoril (Sandoz)
Chemical class	Benzodiazepine
Street name	None

SLEEP MEDICATIONS

Prescription required?	Yes
Available in generic form?	No
Intended use	Hypnotic (sleep-inducer). Not for use in persons under eighteen years.
Dosage form/strength	Capsule, 15 mg, 30 mg
Withdrawal symptoms?	Yes, after stopping medication abruptly, and particularly if taken continuously for several months. May include marked insomnia, convulsions, tremor, muscle cramps.
Side effects	Central nervous system slowdown with degrees of residual daytime drowsiness.
Overdosage effects	Confusion, respiratory depression, coma, hypotension.
Length of action	Intermediate-acting; half-life of 8–38 hours
Precautions *Drug interactions*	Additive effect if taken with alcohol, other central nervous system depressants, antidepressant medication, and antihistamines.
Special at-risk persons	Those over age 60 and persons with liver and kidney disorders have increased susceptibility to daytime hangover reactions and side effects. Pregnant and/or nursing women: avoid use.

Special at-risk persons (continued)	Persons with depression: administer with caution.
	Some types of glaucoma may be worsened.
Habit-forming?	Yes, except for short-term or intermittent use.
Noteworthy	Because of its slow absorption rate, temazepam is inappropriate for those trying to go to sleep more quickly.

TRIAZOLAM

Brand name	Halcion (Upjohn)
Chemical class	Benzodiazepine
Street name	None
Prescription required?	Yes
Available in generic form?	No
Intended use	Hypnotic (sleep inducer). Not for use in persons under eighteen years.
Dosage form	Tablet
Dosage strength	0.25 mg, 0.5 mg
Withdrawal symptoms?	Yes, after stopping medication abruptly. May include significant insomnia, abdominal and muscle cramps, sweating, tremor, convulsions.

Side effects	Central nervous system slowdown with degrees of residual daytime drowsiness
Undesirable effects	Possible memory impairment. Possible early-morning insomnia during period of administration.
Overdosage effects	Severe central nervous system depression, ranging from lethargy to comatose states; respiratory depression; hypotension.
Length of action	Short-acting; half-life of 2–5 hours
Precautions *Drug interactions*	Additive effects if taken with alcohol, other central nervous system depressants, anticonvulsant medication, antidepressant medication, and antihistamines. Cimetidine (Tagamet) taken as ulcer medication may prolong effect of triazolam.
Special at-risk persons	Pregnant and/or nursing women; persons with depression.
Habit-forming?	Dependency likely except for short-term or intermittent use.
Noteworthy	Possible increased wakefulness in last part of night and possible increased daytime anxiety.

PENTOBARBITAL

Brand name	Nembutal (Abbott), U.S.A. Nembutal (Abbott), United Kingdom Nembutal (Abbott), Canada
Chemical class	Barbiturate
Street name	Yellow jackets
Prescription required?	Yes
Available in generic form?	Yes
Intended use	Sedative; short-term hypnotic; pre-anesthetic
Dosage form/strength	Capsule: 50 mg, 100 mg Suppositories
Withdrawal symptoms?	Yes, may include tremor, insomnia, weakness, coma, and death. Prompt recognition and treatment are vital.
Side effects	Central nervous system slowdown; includes degrees of residual daytime drowsiness.
Undesirable effects	Possible skin rash; dizziness; anemia.
Overdosage effects	Severe central nervous system depression, ranging from lethargy to death.
Length of action	Short-acting; half-life of 15–50 hours
Precautions *Drug interactions*	Possibly lethal if alcohol, tranquilizers, antihistamines, seizure medications, or other central nervous system drugs have been taken.

SLEEP MEDICATIONS

Precautions

Drug interactions
(continued)

Interferes with anticoagulant medication, corticosteroids, contraceptive pills, and certain antiepilepsy drugs.

Special at-risk persons

Those over age sixty and persons with severe liver disorders have increased susceptibility to daytime hangover reactions and side effects.

Persons with breathing difficulty: avoid use.

Pregnant and/or nursing women: avoid use.

Monitor children, especially for hyperexcitability.

Habit forming?

Yes, tolerance develops rapidly.

Noteworthy

According to the *New England Journal of Medicine,* "the barbiturate hypnotics have been rendered obsolete by pharmacologic progress and deserve speedy oblivion."

Use of this drug disqualifies user for aircraft piloting.

PHENOBARBITAL

Brand name

At least a dozen trademarked brands

Chemical class

Barbiturate

Street name

Goofballs, purple hearts

Prescription required?	Yes
Available in generic form?	Yes
Intended use	Sedative; sleep medication; seizure disorders
Dosage form	Tablets; elixir; capsules
Dosage strength	Tablets: 8 mg, 15 mg, 30 mg, 60 mg, 100 mg Capsules (timed release): 60 mg Elixir: 20 mg
Withdrawal symptoms?	Yes, may include tremor, insomnia, weakness, delirium, convulsions. Prompt recognition and treatment are vital.
Side effects	Central nervous system slowdown; includes degrees of residual daytime drowsiness.
Undesirable effects	Allergic reactions; dizziness; anemia.
Overdosage effects	Severe central nervous system depression, ranging from lethargy to death.
Length of action	Long-acting; half-life of 3–4 days
Precautions *Drug interactions*	Possibly lethal if alcohol, tranquilizers, antihistamines, seizure medications, or other central nervous system drugs have been taken.

Precautions

    Drug interactions (continued)   Interferes with anticoagulant medication, corticosteroids, contraceptive pills, and certain antiepilepsy drugs, as well as certain antibiotics, quinidine, and griseofulvin.

Special at-risk persons   Those over age sixty and persons with severe liver disease have increased susceptibility to daytime hangover reactions, side effects, and possible hypothermia (lowering of body temperature to below-normal levels).

Pregnant and/or nursing women: avoid use.

Persons with breathing difficulty: avoid use.

Children: do not give to hyperexcitable children. May cause paradoxical reactions (opposite those expected) such as irritability and aggression.

Habit forming?   Yes, tolerance develops rapidly.

Noteworthy   According to the *New England Journal of Medicine,* ''the barbiturate hypnotics have been rendered obsolete by pharmacologic progress and deserve speedy oblivion.''

Use of this drug disqualifies user for aircraft piloting.

A READER'S GUIDE

SECOBARBITAL SODIUM

Brand name	Seconal (Lilly), U.S.A. Seconal (Lilly), United Kingdom Seconal (Lilly), Canada
Chemical class	Barbiturate
Street name	Red devils, reds
Prescription required?	Yes
Available in generic form?	Yes
Intended use	Short-term hypnotic, preanesthetic
Dosage form/strength	Capsule: 50 mg, 100 mg
Withdrawal symptoms?	Yes, may include tremor, insomnia, weakness, coma, and death. Prompt recognition and treatment are vital.
Side effects	Central nervous system slowdown; includes degrees of residual daytime drowsiness.
Undesirable effects	Possible skin rash; dizziness; anemia.
Overdosage effects	Severe central nervous system depression, ranging from lethargy to death.
Length of action	Intermediate-acting; half-life of 15–40 hours
Precautions *Drug interactions*	Possibly lethal if alcohol, tranquilizers, antihistamines, seizure medications, or other central nervous system drugs have been taken.

SLEEP MEDICATIONS

Precautions

Drug interactions (continued)   Interferes with anticoagulant medication, corticosteroids, contraceptive pills, and certain antiepilepsy drugs.

Special at-risk persons   Those over age sixty and persons with severe liver disorders have increased susceptibility to daytime hangover reactions and side effects.

Persons with breathing difficulty: avoid use.

Pregnant and/or nursing women: avoid use.

Monitor children, especially for hyperexcitability.

Habit forming?   Yes, tolerance develops rapidly.

Noteworthy   According to the *New England Journal of Medicine,* "the barbiturate hypnotics have been rendered obsolete by pharmacologic progress and deserve speedy oblivion."

Use of this drug disqualifies user for aircraft piloting.

CHLORAL HYDRATE

Brand name   Noctec (Squibb), U.S.A.
Noctec (Squibb), United Kingdom
Noctec (Squibb), Canada

Popular name   Mickey Finn (combined with alcohol); knockout drops

Prescription required?   Yes

Available in generic form?   Yes

Intended use   Relief of insomnia

Dosage form/strength   Capsules: 250 mg, 500 mg
Elixir, syrup: 250 mg, 500 mg/5 ml (teaspoon)
Suppositories: 500 mg
Use in children limited to no more than one gram given as a single dose.

Withdrawal symptoms?   Yes, often after stopping medication abruptly. May include tremors and anxiety.

Side effects   Central nervous system slowdown; includes degrees of residual daytime drowsiness.

Undesirable effects   Stomach upset; may involve several body systems, particularly central nervous system—causing, for example, headache, dizziness, slurred speech.

Overdosage effects   Severe central nervous system depression, ranging from lethargy to comatose states; diminished reflexes.

Length of action   Intermediate-acting; half-life of six to twelve hours

Precautions
Drug interactions   May briefly interfere with oral anticoagulation medication. Possibly lethal if alcohol, tranquilizers, antihistamines, seizure medications, or other central nervous system drugs have been taken.

Special at-risk persons	Those over age sixty and persons with severe liver disorders have increased susceptibility to daytime hangover reactions and side effects.
	Pregnant and/or nursing women: avoid use.
Habit forming?	Tolerance and dependence develop rapidly.
Noteworthy	Usage of this drug disqualifies user for aircraft piloting. Bad tasting in liquid form. May be swallowed with fruit juice or ginger ale. May give false-positive results in urine glucose testing. Drug effects in the elderly may be mistaken for senility or dementia, leading possibly to inappropriate treatment.

ETHYL ALCOHOL (ETHANOL)

Street names	Booze, hooch
Intended use	Social, recreational
Withdrawal symptoms?	Yes, ranging in severity in susceptible individuals from morning-after hangover, to tremors, weakness, sweating, hallucinations, delirium, coma.
Side effects	Depending on degree of tolerance and duration of intake, depression of central nervous system with initial pseudostimulant effect.
Undesirable effects	May involve several body systems, particularly central nervous system;

Undesirable effects (continued)	irritability, insomnia, nightmares, hallucinations, seizures, confusion, arrhythmias, impaired judgment; high risk of organ damage and/or death; high risk of severe job, family, and interpersonal consequences.
Overdosage effects	Increasing central nervous system depression, ranging from lethargy to comatose states; diminished reflexes

Precautions

Drug interactions	Never safe in combination with most drugs, especially psychoactive ones.
Special at-risk persons	Pregnant and/or nursing women; adolescents.
Habit forming?	Dependency likely; tolerance develops quickly; cross-tolerance to barbiturate and benzodiazepine drugs.

·10·

CONTROLLED SUBSTANCES

In general, the prescribed medications mentioned in these pages—hypnotics, sedatives, analgesics—are psychoactive drugs. In the United States, these are considered substances with abuse potential. They are regulated through five categories, or schedules, of the Controlled Substances Act of 1970. With the exception of the specific exclusion of alcohol and tobacco, each drug is assigned according to its likelihood of being abused, its medical usefulness, and the degree of dependency, if abused.

SCHEDULE I

These substances have no medical use and a high addiction or dependence liability. They may be used legitimately only in government-approved research.

Includes: Heroin
               D-lysergic acid diethylamide (LSD)
               Marijuana

SCHEDULE II

These substances have an accepted medical use but high abuse or dependency potential. The most restrictive of the four medicine schedules, this category requires special security measures, such as vault storage, specific order forms, written prescriptions only, and no automatic refills.

Includes: Narcotics, such as codeine, hydromorphone (Dilaudid), methadone, morphine, opium, and meperidine (Demerol)

Stimulants, such as amphetamines (dextroamphetamine sulfate—Dexedrine), cocaine

Some barbiturates, such as pentobarbital (Nembutal) and secobarbital (Seconal)

SCHEDULE III

These substances have less abuse potential than those in Schedules I and II, have an accepted medical use, and have the possibility that abuse may lead to limited dependency.

Includes: Acetaminophen with codeine
Glutethemide (Doriden)
Methyprylon (Noludar)
Paregoric (tincture of opium)

SCHEDULE IV

These substances have a low potential for abuse compared to those in Schedule III. They have accepted medical uses. Abuse may lead to a limited dependency.

Includes: Benzodiazepines, such as lorazepam (Ativan), chlordiazepoxide (Librium), diazepam (Valium), flurazepam (Dalmane)
Chloral hydrate (Noctec)
Phenobarbital (Luminal)
Propoxyphene (Darvon)

SCHEDULE V

These substances have low potential for abuse, accepted medical usefulness, and abuse may lead to limited dependency.

Includes: Cough preparations with small quantities of narcotic, such as Robitussin A-C
Elixir of Terpin Hydrate with Codeine
Lomotil

·11·
PROFESSIONAL SLEEP ASSOCIATIONS, CLINICS, AND CENTERS

The American Narcolepsy Association, Inc.
Box 5846
Stanford, CA 94305

Association of Sleep Disorder Centers
P.O. Box 2604
Del Mar, CA 92014

The Association of Sleep Disorders Centers, founded in 1975, has a membership of both accredited and provisionally accredited centers. The specialty sleep laboratory is a recent category of sleep center. This classification refers to a sleep center that specializes in particular sleep disorders, such as sleep apnea, or the sleep problems of children.

At the time of this publication, it is likely that many of the following provisional members will be fully accredited. Over the past one and one-half years, the membership has significantly grown.

ACCREDITED CENTERS

ALABAMA
Sleep Disorders Center of
  Alabama
Affiliated with Baptist Medical
  Center Montclair
800 Montclair Road
Birmingham, AL 35213
Attn: Vernon Pegram, Ph.D.
(205) 592-5650

ARIZONA
Sleep Disorders Center
Good Samaritan Medical
  Center
1111 East McDowell Road
Phoenix, AZ 85006
Attn: Richard M. Riedy, M.D.
(602) 239-5815

Sleep Disorders Center
University of Arizona
1501 North Campbell Avenue
Tucson, AZ 85724
Attn: Stuart F. Quan, M.D.
(602) 626-6112

CALIFORNIA
Sleep Disorders Center
Scripps Clinic and Research
  Foundation
10666 North Torrey
  Pines Road
La Jolla, CA 92037
Attn: Richard M. Timms, M.D.
(619) 455-8087

UCLA Sleep Disorders Clinic
Department of Neurology
Westwood Plaza, Room
  1184 RNRC
Los Angeles, CA 90024
Attn: Emery Zimmermann,
  M.D., Ph.D.
(213) 206-8005

Sleep Disorders Center
Holy Cross Hospital
15031 Rinaldi Street
Mission Hills, CA 91345
Attn: Elliott R. Phillips, M.D.
(818) 898-4639

Sleep Disorders Center
U.C. Irvine Medical Center
101 City Drive South
Orange, CA 92668
Attn: Jon Sassin, M.D.
(714) 634-5777

Sleep Disorders Center
Sequoia Hospital
Whipple and Alameda
Redwood City, CA 94062
Attn: Drs. Votteri and Pavy
(415) 367-5620

Sleep Disorders Program
Department of Psychiatry
  TD114
Stanford University School of
  Medicine
Stanford, CA 94305
Attn: German Nino-Murcia, M.D.
(415) 497-6601

COLORADO
Sleep Disorders Center
Presbyterian Medical Center
1719 East 19th Avenue
Denver, CO 80218
Attn: Ian Happer, M.D.
(303) 839-6447

Sleep Disorders Center
University of Colorado Health
  Sciences Center
700 Delaware Street
Denver, CO 80204
Attn: Drs. Reite and Zimmerman
(303) 394-7743

CONNECTICUT
Sleep Disorders Center
The Griffin Hospital
130 Division Street
Derby, CT 06418
Attn: Drs. Sewitch and
  Liebmann
(203) 735-7421

FLORIDA
Sleep Disorders Center
Mt. Sinai Medical Center
4300 Alton Road
Miami Beach, FL 33140
Attn: Martin A. Cohn, M.D.
(305) 674-2613

GEORGIA
Sleep Disorders Center
Northside Hospital
1000 Johnson Ferry Road

Atlanta, GA 30342
Attn: James J. Wellman,
  M.D.
(404) 256-8977

HAWAII
Sleep Disorders Center
Straub Clinic and Hospital
888 South King Street
Honolulu, HI 96813
Attn: James W. Pearce, M.D.
(808) 523-2311 x8448

ILLINOIS
Sleep Disorders Center
Rush-Presbyterian-St. Luke's
1753 West Congress Parkway
Chicago, IL 60612
Attn: Rosalind Cartwright,
  Ph.D.
(312) 942-5440

Sleep Disorders Center
University of Chicago
5841 South Maryland Avenue
  Box 425
Chicago, IL 60637
Attn: Jean-Paul Spire, M.D.
(312) 962-1780

Sleep Disorders Center
Methodist Medical Center of
  Illinois
221 N.E. Glen Oak
Peoria, IL 61636
Attn: Drs. Morgan and Lee
(309) 672-4966

KENTUCKY
Sleep Disorders Center
Humana Hospital Audubon
One Audubon Plaza Drive
Louisville, KY 40217
Attn: Carl P. Browman, Ph.D.
(502) 636-7459

LOUISIANA
Tulane Sleep Disorders Center
Department of Psychiatry and
    Neurology
1415 Tulane Avenue
New Orleans, LA 70112
Attn: Gregory Ferriss, M.D.
(504) 588-5231

MARYLAND
Sleep Disorders Center
Francis Scott Key Hospital
Johns Hopkins School of Medi-
    cine
Baltimore, MD 21224
Attn: Richard Allen, Ph.D.
(301) 955-0571

National Capital Sleep Center
4520 East West Highway
Number 406
Bethesda, MD 20814
Attn: Wallace B. Mendelson, M.D.
(301) 656-9515

MICHIGAN
Sleep Disorders Center
Henry Ford Hospital
2799 West Grand Boulevard
Detroit, MI 48202
Attn: Frank Zorick, M.D.
(313) 972-1800

MINNESOTA
Sleep Disorders Center
Methodist Hospital
6500 Excelsior Boulevard
Minneapolis, MN 55426
Attn: Mark K. Wedel, M.D.
(612) 932-6083

Sleep Disorders Center
Neurology Department
Hennepin County Medical
    Center
Minneapolis, MN 55415
Attn: Mark Mahowald, M.D.
(612) 347-6288

Sleep Disorders Center
Mayo Clinic
200 First Street, S.W.
Rochester, MN 55905
Attn: Philip R. Westbrook,
    M.D.
(507) 285-4150

MISSOURI
Sleep Disorders Center
St. Louis University Medical
    Center
1221 South Grand Boulevard
St. Louis, MO 63104
Attn: Kristyna M. Hartse,
    Ph.D.
(314) 557-8704

Sleep Disorders Center
Deaconess Hospital
6150 Oakland Avenue
St. Louis, MO 63139
Attn: James K. Walsh, Ph.D.
(314) 768-3100

NEW HAMPSHIRE
Sleep Disorders Center
Department of Psychiatry
Dartmouth Medical School
Hanover, NH 03756
Attn: Michael Sateia, M.D.
(603) 646-7521

NEW YORK
Sleep-Wake Disorders Center
Montefiore Hospital
111 East 210th Street
Bronx, NY 10467
Attn: Michael J. Thorpy, M.D.
(212) 920-4841

Sleep Disorders Center
Columbia-Presbyterian Medical
    Center
161 Fort Washington Avenue
New York, NY 10032
Attn: Neil B. Kavey, M.D.
(212) 305-1860

Sleep Disorders Center
St. Mary's Hospital
89 Genesee Street
Rochester, NY 14611
Attn: Donald W. Greenblatt, M.D.
(716) 464-3391

Sleep Disorders Center
Department of Psychiatry
SUNY at Stony Brook
Stony Brook, NY 11794
Attn: Theodore L. Baker, Ph.D.
(516) 444-2916

Sleep-Wake Disorders Center
New York Hospital-Cornell
    Med. Ctr.

21 Bloomingdale Road
White Plains, NY 10605
Attn: Charles Pollak, M.D.
(914) 997-5751

OHIO
Sleep Disorders Center
Jewish Hospital
515 Melish Avenue
Cincinnati, OH 45229
Attn: Martin B. Scharf, Ph.D.
(513) 861-7770

Sleep Disorders Center
Department of Neurology
Cleveland Clinic
Cleveland, OH 44106
Attn: Dudley S. Dinner, M.D.
(216) 444-8732

Sleep Disorders Evaluation Center
Department of Psychiatry
Ohio State University
Columbus, OH 43210
Attn: Helmut S. Schmidt, M.D.
(614) 421-8296

OKLAHOMA
Sleep Disorders Center
Presbyterian Hospital
N.E. 13th at Lincoln Boulevard
Oklahoma City, OK 73104
Attn: William Orr, Ph.D.
(405) 271-6312

OREGON
Sleep Disorders Program
Good Samaritan Hospital

2222 N.W. Lovejoy Street
Portland, OR 97210
Attn: Gerald B. Rich, M.D.
(503) 229-8311

PENNSYLVANIA

Sleep Disorders Center
The Medical College of
    Pennsylvania
3300 Henry Avenue
Philadelphia, PA 19129
Attn: June M. Fry, Ph.D., M.D.
(215) 842-4250

Sleep Disorders Center
Western Psychiatric Institute
3811 O'Hara Street
Pittsburgh, PA 15213
Attn: Charles F. Reynolds, III,
    M.D.
(412) 624-2246

Sleep Disorders Center
Department of Neurology
Crozer-Chester Medical
    Center
Upland - Chester, PA 19013
Attn: Calvin Stafford, M.D.
(215) 447-2689

TENNESSEE

BMH Sleep Disorders Center
Baptist Memorial Hospital
899 Madison Avenue
Memphis, TN 38146
Attn: Helio Lemmi, M.D.
(901) 522-5704

Sleep Disorders Center
Saint Thomas Hospital

P.O. Box 380
Nashville, TN 37202
Attn: J. Brevard Haynes, Jr., M.D.
(615) 386-2066

TEXAS

Sleep-Wake Disorders Center
Presbyterian Hospital
8200 Walnut Hill Lane
Dallas, TX 75231
Attn: Howard P. Roffwarg, M.D.
(214) 696-8563

Sleep Disorders Center
All Saints Episcopal Hospital
1400 8th Avenue
Forth Worth, TX 76101
Attn: Edgar Lucas, Ph.D.
(817) 927-6120

Sleep Disorders Center
Department of Psychiatry
Baylor College of Medicine
Houston, TX 77030
Attn: Ismet Karacan, M.D.
(713) 799-4886

Sleep Disorders Center
Humana Hospital Metropolitan
1303 McCullough
San Antonio, TX 78212
Attn: Sabri Derman, M.D.
(512) 223-4057

Sleep Disorders Center
Scott and White Clinic
2401 South 31st Street
Temple, TX 76508
Attn: Francisco Perez-Guerra,
    M.D.
(817) 774-2554

UTAH
Intermountain Sleep Disorders
  Center
LDS Hospital

325 8th Avenue
Salt Lake City, UT 84143
Attn: Drs. Walker and Farney
(801) 321-1378

ACCREDITED SPECIALTY LABORATORIES FOR SLEEP-RELATED BREATHING DISORDERS

CALIFORNIA
Sleep Apnea Center
Merritt-Peralta Medical Center
450 30th Street
Oakland, CA 94609
Attn: Drs. Kram and Nusser
(415) 451-4900 x2273

Southern California Sleep Apnea
  Center
Lombard Medical Group
2230 Lynn Road

Thousand Oaks, CA 91360
Attn: Ronald A. Popper, M.D.
(805) 495-1066

PENNSYLVANIA
Sleep Disorders Center
Mercy Hospital of Johnstown
1127 Franklin Street
Johnstown, PA 15905
Attn: Drs. Hanzel and Parcinski
(814) 533-1000

PROVISIONAL MEMBERS

ALABAMA
Sleep Disorders Center
The Children's Hospital of
  Alabama
1600 7th Avenue South
Birmingham, AL 35233
Attn: Drs. Wooten and Lyrene
(205) 939-9386

Sleep/Wake Disorders Center
University of Alabama

University Station
Birmingham, AL 35294
Attn: Drs. Wooten and
  Faught
(205) 934-7110

North Alabama Sleep Disorders
  Center
Huntsville Hospital
101 Sivley Road
Huntsville, AL 35801

Attn: Paul Legrand, M.D.
(205) 533-8020

ARKANSAS
Sleep Disorders Center
Baptist Medical Center
9601 I-630 Exit 7
Little Rock, AR 72205-7299
Attn: Drs. Galbraith and Phillips
(501) 227-4750

Sleep Disorders Diagnostic and
    Research Center
University of Arkansas for
    Medical Sciences
4301 West Markham, Slot 555
Little Rock, AR 72205
Attn: Drs. Scrima and Hiller
(501) 661-5528

CALIFORNIA
WMCA Sleep Disorders Center
Western Medical Center -
    Anaheim
1025 South Anaheim Boulevard
Anaheim, CA 92805
Attn: Louis McNabb, M.D.
(714) 491-1159

Sleep Disorders Center
Downey Community Hospital
11500 Brookshire Avenue
Downey, CA 90241
Attn: Mark J. Buchfuhrer, M.D.
(213) 806-5280

Sleep Disorders Institute
St. Jude Hospital and
    Rehabilitation Center

101 East Valencia Mesa Drive
Fullerton, CA 92634
Attn: Drs. Roethe, Sturman and
    Petrie
(714) 871-3280

Sleep Disorders Center
Palma Intercommunity Hospital
7901 Walker Street
La Palma, CA 90623
Attn: Joel B. Younger, M.D.
(714) 522-0150

Loma Linda Sleep Disorders
    Center
Loma Linda University Medical
    Center
11234 Anderson Street
Loma Linda, CA 92354
Attn: Michael Bonnet, Ph.D.
(714) 825-7084 x2703

Sleep Disorders Center
Hollywood Presbyterian
    Medical Center
1300 North Vermont Street
Los Angeles, CA 90027
Attn: Drs. McGinty and Rothfeld
(213) 660-3530

Sleep Disorders Center
The Hospital of the Good
    Samaritan
616 South Witmer Street
Los Angeles, CA 90017
Attn: F. Grant Buckle, M.D.
(213) 977-2206

Sleep Disorders Center
Pomona Valley Community
    Hospital

1798 North Garey Avenue
Pomona, CA 91767
Attn: Drs. Zinke and Desai
(714) 623-8715 x2135

Sleep Disorders Clinic and
    Research Center
St. Mary's Hospital
450 Stanyan Street
San Francisco, CA 94117
Attn: Drs. Nevins and Derman
(415) 750-5579

Sleep Disorders Center
San Jose Hospital
675 East Santa Clara Street
San Jose, CA 95112
Attn: Drs. Choslovsky and
    Connor
(408) 977-4445

Sleep Disorders Center
South Coast Medical Center
31872 Coast Highway
South Laguna, CA 92677
Attn: Drs. Pittluck and de Berry
(714) 499-1311 x2186

Sleep Disorders Center
Torrance Memorial Hospital
3330 Lomita Boulevard
Torrance, CA 90509
Attn: Lawrence W. Kneisley,
    M.D.
(213) 325-9110 x2049

COLORADO
Porter Regional Sleep Disorders
    Center
Porter Memorial Hospital

2525 South Downing
Denver, CO 80210
Attn: Richard Mountain, M.D.
(303) 778-5723

CONNECTICUT
New Haven Sleep Disorders
    Center
100 York Street
Suite 2 G
New Haven, CT 06511
Attn: Drs. Watson and
    Sholomskas
(203) 776-9578

DISTRICT OF
COLUMBIA
Sleep Disorders Center
Georgetown University Hospital
3800 Reservoir Road, N.W.
Washington, D.C. 20007
Attn: Samuel J. Potolicchio, Jr.,
    M.D.
(202) 625-2697 x2020

FLORIDA
Sleep Disorders Center
Sacred Heart Hospital
5151 North 9th Avenue
Pensacola, FL 32504
Attn: Frank V. Messina, M.D.
(904) 476-7851 x4128

IOWA
Sleep Disorders Center
Iowa Methodist Medical Center
1200 Pleasant Street

Des Moines, IA 50308
Attn: Randall R. Hanson, M.D.
(515) 283-6207

Sleep Disorders Center
Department of Neurology
University of Iowa Hospitals and
   Clinics
Iowa City, IA 52242
Attn: Quentin Stokes Dickens,
   M.D.
(319) 356-2571

IDAHO
Idaho Sleep Disorders Center
St. Luke's Regional Medical
   Center
190 East Bannock
Boise, ID 83712
Attn: Bruce T. Adornato, M.D.
(208) 386-2440

ILLINOIS
Henrotin Sleep Disorders Center
Henrotin Hospital
111 West Oak Street
Chicago, IL 60610
Attn: R. A. Gross, M.D.
(312) 440-7777

Sleep Disorders Center
Neurology Service
Veterans Hospital
Hines, IL 60141
Attn: Meenal Mamdani, M.D.
(312) 343-7200 x2326

Sleep Disorders Clinic and
   Laboratory

Carle Clinic and Hospital
611 West Park Street
Urbana, IL 61801
Attn: Drs. Picchietti and Greeley
(217) 337-3364

INDIANA
Sleep Disorders Center
St. Mary's Medical Center
3700 Washington Avenue
Evansville, IN 47750
Attn: David Howard, M.D.
(812) 479-4257

Regional Sleep Studies Laboratory
The Lutheran Hospital of Fort
   Wayne, Inc.
3024 Fairfield Avenue
Fort Wayne, IN 46807
Attn: Bruce J. Hopen, M.D.
(219) 458-2001

Sleep Disorders Center
Winona Memorial Hospital
3232 North Meridian Street
Indianapolis, IN 46208
Attn: Frederick A. Tolle, M.D.
(317) 927-2100

Sleep Disorders Center
Lafayette Home Hospital
2400 South Street
Lafayette, IN 47903
Attn: Fredrick Robinson, M.D.
(317) 447-6811

KANSAS
Sleep Disorders Center
Wesley Medical Center

550 North Hillside
Wichita, KS 67214
Attn: Arnold M. Barnett,
    M.R.C.P., F.A.C.P.
(316) 688-2660

KENTUCKY
Sleep Disorders Center
St. Joseph's Hospital
1 St. Joseph Drive
Lexington, KY 40504
Attn: Robert Granacher, Jr.,
    M.D.
(606) 278-3436

Sleep Disorders Center
Good Samaritan Hospital
310 South Limestone
Lexington, KY 40508
Attn: George W. Privett, Jr.,
    M.D.
(606) 278-0352

LOUISIANA
Sleep Disorders Center
Touro Infirmary
1401 Foucher
New Orleans, LA 70115
Attn: Gihan Kader, M.D.
(504) 891-7087

Sleep Disorders Center
Willis-Knighton Medical
    Center
2600 Greenwood Road
Shreveport, LA 71103
Attn: Nabil A. Moufarrej,
    M.D.
(318) 632-4823

MASSACHUSETTS
Sleep Disorders Center
Boston University Medical
    Center
75 East Newton Street
Boston, MA 02146
Attn: George F. Howard, III, M.D.
(617) 247-5206

Sleep Disorders Center
Boston Children's Hospital
300 Longwood Avenue
Boston, MA 02115
Attn: Richard Ferber, M.D.
(617) 735-6242

Sleep Disorders Unit
Harvard University School of
    Medicine
Beth Israel Hospital - 330
    Brookline Avenue
Boston, MA 02215
Attn: June Matheson, M.D.
(617) 735-3237

Sleep-Wake Disorders Unit
University of Massachusetts
55 Lake Avenue North
Worcester, MA 01605
Attn: Sandra Horowitz, M.D.
(617) 856-3802

MICHIGAN
Sleep Disorders Center
University of Michigan Medical
    Center
1405 East Ann Street
Ann Arbor, MI 48109
Attn: Michael S. Aldrich, M.D.
(313) 763-5118

Sleep Disorders Center
Ingham Medical Center
401 West Greenlawn Avenue
Lansing, MI 48909
Attn: Samuel M. McMahon, M.D.
(517) 374-2333

MINNESOTA
Sleep Disorders Center
Fairview Southdale Hospital
6401 France Avenue, South
Edina, MN 55435
Attn: Drs. Corson and Zarling
(612) 924-5058

MISSOURI
Sleep Disorders Center
St. Mary's Hospital
101 Memorial Drive
Kansas City, MO 64108
Attn: Iftekhar Ahmed, M.D.
(816) 756-2651

Sleep Disorders Center
Research Medical Center
2316 East Meyer Boulevard
Kansas City, MO 64132-1199
Attn: Ronald Chisholm, Ph.D.
(816) 276-4222

MISSISSIPPI
Sleep Disorders Center
Division of Somnology
University of Mississippi
Jackson, MS 39216
Attn: Lawrence S. Schoen,
    Ph.D.
(601) 987-5552

NORTH CAROLINA
Sleep Disorders Center
Charlotte Memorial Hospital
P. O. Box 32861
Charlotte, NC 28232
Attn: Dennis Hill, M.D.
(704) 331-2121

Sleep Disorders Center
Division of Neurology
Duke University Medical Center
Durham, NC 27710
Attn: J. Scott Luther, M.D.
(919) 684-6003

NORTH DAKOTA
TNI Sleep Disorders Center
St. Luke's Hospital
5th Street at Mills Avenue
Fargo, ND 58102
Attn: Philip M. Becker, M.D.
(701) 280-5673

NEBRASKA
Sleep Disorders Center
Lutheran Medical Center
515 South 26th Street
Omaha, NE 68103
Attn: Drs. Ellingson and Roehrs
(402) 536-6352

NEW HAMPSHIRE
Sleep-Wake Disorders Center
Hampstead Hospital
East Road
Hampstead, NH 03841
Attn: J. Gila Lindsley, Ph.D.
(603) 329-5311 x240

NEW JERSEY
Sleep Disorders Center
Newark Beth Israel Medical
    Center
201 Lyons Avenue
Newark, NJ 07112
Attn: Monroe S. Karetzky, M.D.
(201) 926-7597

NEW MEXICO
Sleep Disorders Center
Lovelace Medical Center
5400 Gibson Boulevard S.E.
Albuquerque, NM 87108
Attn: Fernando G. Miranda,
    M.D.
(505) 262-7250

NEW YORK
Sleep Disorders Center
Winthrop-University Hospital
259 First Street
Mineola, NY 11501
Attn: Alan M. Fein, M.D.
(516) 663-2005

Institute for Sleep and Aging
Mount Sinai Medical Center
One Gustave Levy Place
New York, NY 10129
Attn: Charles Herrera, M.D.
(212) 650-5561

OHIO
Sleep Disorders Center
Bethesda Oak Hospital
619 Oak Street

Cincinnati, OH 45206
Attn: Milton Kramer, M.D.
(513) 569-6320

Northwest Ohio Sleep Disorders
    Center
The Toledo Hospital
2142 North Cove Boulevard
Toledo, OH 43606
Attn: Frank O. Horton, III,
    M.D.
(419) 471-5629

OKLAHOMA
Sleep Disorders Center
Saint Francis Hospital
6161 South Yale
Tulsa, OK 74136
Attn: Richard M. Bregman, M.D.
(918) 494-1350

PENNSYLVANIA
Sleep Disorders Center
Jefferson Medical College
1015 Walnut Street, Third
    Floor
Philadelphia, PA 19107
Attn: Karl Doghramji, M.D.
(215) 928-6175

SOUTH CAROLINA
Sleep Disorders Center
Baptist Medical Center
Taylor at Marion Streets
Columbia, SC 29220
Attn: Drs. Bogan and Ellis
(803) 771-5557

PROFESSIONAL SLEEP CENTERS

TENNESSEE
Sleep Disorders Center
Fort Sanders Regional Medical
 Center
1901 West Clinch Avenue
Knoxville, TN 37916
Attn: Ronald W. Bryan, M.D.
(615) 971-1375

Sleep Disorders Center
St. Mary's Medical Center
Oak Hill Avenue
Knoxville, TN 37917
Attn: Michael L. Eisenstadt,
 M.D.
(615) 971-6011

TEXAS
Sleep Disorders Center
Sun Towers Hospital
1801 North Oregon
El Paso, TX 79902
Attn: Gonzalo Diaz, M.D.
(915) 532-6281

Sleep Disorders Center
Sam Houston Memorial
 Hospital
1624 Pech, P.O. Box 55130
Houston, TX 77055
Attn: Todd Swick, M.D.
(713) 468-4311

Sleep Disorders Center
Pasadena Bayshore Medical
 Center
4000 Spencer Highway
Pasadena, TX 71504
Attn: Drs. Bradley and Stein
(713) 944-6666

UTAH
Sleep Disorders Center
Utah Neurological Clinic
1999 North Columbia Lane
Provo, UT 84604
Attn: John M. Andrews, M.D.
(801) 226-2300

VIRGINIA
Sleep Disorders Center
Norfolk General Hospital
600 Gresham Drive
Norfolk, VA 23507
Attn: Reuben H. McBrayer, M.D.
(804) 628-3322

Sleep Disorders Center
Community Hospital of
 Roanoke Valley
P. O. Box 12946
Roanoke, VA 24029
Attn: Thomas W. DeBeck, M.D.
(703) 985-8435

WASHINGTON
Sleep Disorders Center
Providence Medical Center
500 17th Avenue C-34008
Seattle, WA 98124
Attn: Ralph A. Pascualy, M.D.
(206) 326-5366

WISCONSIN
Sleep Disorders Center
Gundersen Clinic, Ltd.
1836 South Avenue
La Crosse, WI 54601
Attn: Larry A. Lindesmith, M.D.
(608) 782-7300

Sleep Disorders Center
Columbia Hospital
2025 East Newport Avenue
Milwaukee, WI 53211
Attn: Paul A. Nausieda, M.D.
(414) 961-4650

Sleep Disorders Center
Milwaukee Children's Hospital
1700 West Wisconsin Avenue
Milwaukee, WI 53201
Attn: Thomas B. Rice, M.D.
(414) 931-4016

·12·
THE LANGUAGE OF SLEEP:
AN ANNOTATED GLOSSARY

Insomnia is so common a symptom that many people uncritically refer to their sleep problems, whatever they may be, as insomnia. This lack of precision in language, its very casualness, can easily become a barrier to good medical care. Medicine, at all costs, must avoid the Alice-in-Wonderland syndrome:

"When I use a word," Humpty Dumpty said, in rather a scornful tone, "it means just what I choose it to mean . . ."

Lewis Carroll, *Through the Looking Glass*

Being a patient within the medical-care system can not only bring many health benefits but can also deliver a measure of frustration and misunderstanding, if the words used are not clear to you. The new idiom of the new specialty—sleep medicine—has spawned a new vocabulary. Technical definitions may be a requirement for scientists, but the rest of us might welcome the kind of popular interpretations that follow.

ABUSE. In clinical medicine, a repetitive habitual behavior pattern of compulsively ingesting drugs. Most commonly refers to psychoactive drugs.

ADDICTION. An overpowering and repeated craving for a drug, according to the World Health Organization, is one measure of addiction. In addition, other indications include quick development of tolerance to the drug's effects and the appearance of withdrawal symptoms when the drug is suddenly stopped.

ADMINISTRATION. Used often in health care to specify the delivery to a patient of food, fluids, and other nursing care requirements.

ALPHA WAVES. The brain-wave pattern characteristic in polygraph tracings of a resting, relaxed subject. The pattern is commonly seen in the earliest stage of sleep and may also be present during the relaxed wakefulness of biofeedback and transcendental meditation.

ANALGESIA. Refers broadly to a feeling of relief from pain. It is basically a diminished awareness of pain. That is, the painful condition itself may not be changed, but your reaction to it has altered. It is less intrusive in your consciousness. The range of therapies directed toward creating this feeling is widespread: medications, biofeedback, psychological strategies, exercise, electronic stimulation.

AROUSAL. A brain function in which the ability to switch from a less alert level of consciousness to a more alert one is triggered, such as from sleeping to wakefulness.

BASELINE. The starting point for any kind of sequential studies; intended to be the first of a series of observations and comparisons.

BENZODIAZEPINE. A family of drugs—all psychoactive—from which are chosen some of the most commonly used medications for insomnia, such as flurazepam (Dalmane) and lorazepam (Ativan).

BIOAVAILABILITY. Refers to the rate and completeness of release within the body of the active ingredients in a drug. The generic drug versus trademark drug controversy has spotlighted the concept of bioavailability. The debate arises from purported differences between generic and proprietary products regarding this release, that is, whether two such products are equally effective, or bioequivalent. The line of reasoning is this: If the bioavailability of a drug varies from manufacturer to manufacturer, or even within batches produced by the same manufacturer, then the therapeutic effect cannot be predicted with certainty. Consumer groups and drug manufacturers are lined up on opposite sides, with the Food and Drug Administration—responsible for standards of drug safety, strength, purity, and effectiveness—practicing physicians, and pharmacists caught in the middle.

BIOFEEDBACK. A compound word with both scientific and mathematical origins. It is both a concept and a technique whereby you are able to gauge some of your body's involuntary activities, such as blood pressure, heartbeat, or temperature. From this information, many people have learned to change their body responses in a beneficial way.

BIORHYTHMS. Refers to biological rhythms, such as the alternation of sleep and wakefulness, or the contraction and expansion of a beating heart. The disorders in this "timing" system can cause sleep problems, and is the focus of the science of chronobiology.

CHRONOBIOLOGY. As used in sleep clinics, the organized study of human biological rhythms, of which the sleep-wake cycle is one of many, based fundamentally on a twenty-four-hour day-night "clock." A common application is in jet lag, when body or biological rhythm time is "out of phase" with clock time.

CHRONOTHERAPY. Refers specifically to an insomnia treatment that aligns your sleep-wake rhythm to the prevailing light-dark hours of your environment. A person who has had longstanding difficulty falling asleep before 2 or 3 A.M. can progressively delay bedtime by three-hour steps. Doing this each twenty-four-hour period, or progressing on a weekly basis, the bedtime is eventually moved around the clock to the desired hour of slumber.

CIRCADIAN RHYTHM. *Circa* in Latin means "around" and *dies* means "day." Together they refer to biological rhythm patterns of twenty-four hours, plus or minus one or two hours.

CROSS-TOLERANCE. The development of tolerance in a person who is already tolerant to other drugs in the same chemical family.

DELTA WAVES. This brain wave pattern basically denotes deep sleep; also called stages 3 and 4 of non-REM sleep.

DEPENDENCY. A preventable, treatable illness characterized by a persistent need of a substance to restore a sense of ease. Pill dependency affects one out of ten people—often without their knowing it.

DEPRESSANTS. A class of drugs which slow down both physical activity and mental capabilities. Mood changes inversely parallel dosage changes and as the ingested dosage increases, body movement decreases. The end results of rising overdosage are coma and death. So many of the effects of a common group of depressants, barbiturates, are such mirror images of alcohol that the one substance, alcohol, has been called liquid barbiturate, and the other, solid alcohol. Alcohol is bought and sold as a nondrug, whereas barbiturates are treated as controlled substances subject to numerous legal restraints.

DRUG. Frequently used to refer to a medication; sometimes used to mean a substance that produces a sedative effect or a hypnotic (sleep-inducing) effect; also used as a street name for illicit substances; occasionally used as a verb to describe the action of causing someone to progressively diminish his or her awareness.

DRUG HOLIDAY. Planned periods in a medication schedule during which time medication is withheld. This drug-free period helps reduce the possible development of tolerance and dependency as well as minimize side effects.

ECG (also EKG). Electrocardiogram. A tracing of the electrical activity of the heart.

EEG. Electroencephalogram. A tracing of the electrical activity of the brain.

EMG. Electromyography. Measuring the electrical activity associated with selected muscle movement.

EOG. Electro-oculogram. A tracing measuring the electrical activity associated with eye movements.

ERECTILE DISORDER. Usually refers to inability of adult males to have or maintain an erection. The NPT (nocturnal penile tumescence) studies that are carried out in the sleep laboratory are a helpful technique to assist in the differential diagnosis between organic and psychogenic causes of impotence.

GENERIC DRUGS. Described in several ways, all of which must be considered together for an accurate and useful assessment of your medication:
Chemistry. The names of generic drugs are derived from—and are usually shortened versions of—the longer chemical molecular name.

The generic name and the proprietary name of the same drug are different, such as lorazepam (Ativan).

Marketing. Generic drugs are marketed through a generic pharmaceutical manufacturing company or a specific division of an established drug house. Generics can be offered to the consumer only after the owner's patent has expired on the proprietary medication.

Cost. Generic drugs are usually less expensive than their trademarked counterparts.

HALF-LIFE. In clinical practice, refers essentially to how quickly or slowly a drug can be eliminated from your body. That is, the length of time for 50 percent of a dose to be cleared from the bloodstream. Many variables affect the length of time a drug remains therapeutically active in your body: for example, age, body weight, hormonal and nutritional status, sex, pregnancy, genetic differences, concurrent diseases, diet, environmental exposures. For this reason, the single number of hours usually given as a specific half-life must be considered only approximate, particularly as these numbers have been derived from studies on healthy young adults.

HYPNAGOGIC HALLUCINATION. Refers to dreams or intense reveries straddling the boundary between wakefulness and sleep. These auditory and visual experiences frequently occur during the onset of sleep, reflecting a sequence that is not found in normal sleep, when the dreaming phase, or REM, begins after approximately ninety minutes.

HYPNOTIC. In general, refers to those drugs—all psychoactive—intended to promote sleep. The word is sometimes used interchangeably with sedative or tranquilizer. To be precise, however, there is a difference, and that is one of dosage. A drug that acts as a hypnotic at a particular dose will act as a sedative—without causing sleep—when given in smaller divided doses.

JET LAG (see Chronobiology)

INSOMNIA. A repeated symptom of disordered ability to sleep and wake in a balanced pattern, which previously provided a feeling of satisfactory rest and capable activity. Clinical medicine uses additional descriptive terms—transient insomnia (for two or three weeks) or chronic insomnia (months or years)—to convey duration of this symptom; or drug-dependency insomnia to name repeatedly misused substances (such as sleeping pills) as the cause.

INTERACTION. The effects produced by the use of more than one drug. When you are taking more than one medication, the therapeutic effects and side effects may be changed from when either drug is taken alone. Similarly, alcohol and some foods can alter the anticipated reactions to medication—for example, alcohol has a multiplier effect on sleeping pills.

L-TRYPTOPHAN.   An amino acid that is part of the normal chemistry of the brain and is present in certain foods, such as milk. Claims have been made for its ability to induce sleep, but these have not been proven.

NARCOLEPSY.   A sleep disorder characterized by two or more of the following conditions:

• Brief, repetitive daytime attacks of uncontrollable sleepiness, in spite of a general background of chronic drowsiness.
• Cataplexy, in which emotional expressions such as laughter or a sense of surprise precede a sudden, brief, involuntary muscle paralysis, perhaps only a few seconds long.
• Sleep paralysis, in which an inability to move seems to overcome the sufferer, either on falling asleep or awakening; can last several seconds to a few minutes.
• Hypnogogic hallucinations may occur as vivid dreams and are sometimes experienced during full consciousness.

NARCOTIC.   Synonymous with the term opiate. Opiates are, strictly speaking, derivatives of the opium poppy. Nonopiate synthetic narcotics act in a similar manner. Narcotics—most importantly opium, morphine, heroin, and codeine—are used medically to relieve pain, sedate, promote sleep, and alleviate coughing and diarrhea. Street abuse of and addiction to narcotics are common; however, rationally prescribed analgesic use usually does not lead to addiction.

NPT (NOCTURNAL PENILE TUMESCENCE).   The natural enlargement of the penis during certain sleep phases. The inability to experience erections when awake may be due to psychological, anatomical, or hormonal reasons, or a combination. Sleep experts have learned that polysomnographic recordings of the sleeper can be used to help diagnosis the origins of his impotence.

NON-REM.   An acronym for the period of sleep during which there is no rapid eye movement beneath the closed lids. Also called S sleep (synchronized sleep) and orthodox sleep. Non-REM sleep consists of successively deeper sleep periods, which have been called stages 1, 2, 3, and 4, or alternatively, 1, 2, and delta sleep.

OVER-THE-COUNTER. A medication purchase without a doctor's prescription. The active ingredient in the over-the-counter sleep aids is usually an antihistamine.

PLACEBO. A nonmedicinal substance that appears to be a medication. The "placebo effect" implies belief by the user that a bland "sugar pill" is in fact an effective medication.

POLYSOMNOGRAPH. Usually refers to a group of electronic instruments, attached to a person, and used to sense and record the electrical activity of the brain, the eyes, and certain muscles during sleep. Also refers to the inked tracings—polysomnograms—made by the various instruments. Can be used to describe the process whereby tracing recordings are generated, to be later studied by an expert. Similar to a heart specialist reading an electrocardiogram, the sleep expert reads the wavy lines and squiggles of the recordings, which indicate exactly such important data as the time of falling asleep, length of various sleep stages, number of wake periods, and number of dream periods.

PSYCHOACTIVE, PSYCHOTROPIC. Refers to substances, such as tranquilizers, stimulants, and hypnotics (sleeping pills), as well as alcohol, that provoke changes in mood and behavior by depression or stimulation of the central nervous system. Psychoactive substances can alter mind-body processes, such as alertness, perception of reality, memory, sleep-wake patterns, and the vital brain centers regulating breathing and heartbeat.

REBOUND INSOMNIA. A drug reaction consisting of a return of the original symptoms of insomnia, or more probably a worsening of symptoms, when sleep medication is abruptly discontinued. Some doctors are experimenting with a "drug holiday" schedule in which the medication is used, stopped, then used again at monitored trial intervals.

REM. An acronym referring to rapid eye movement beneath closed lids, occurring during alternating intervals of sleep. Most dreaming occurs during this period of sleep, a time of much physiological activity within the body. In normal sleep, REM sleep follows the non-REM period and alternates with it. (Not to be confused with the medical radiology term rem, which is a measure of radiation exposure.)

SEDATIVE. A general category of central nervous system depressant medications that not only diminish a feeling of apprehension but can also reduce a sense of pain and may help encourage sleep. Sedative properties—that is, diminished awareness of the environment, lethargy, drowsiness—are characteristically found in many psychotropics, including antihistamines and narcotic analgesics. The impression that sedation is a deeper form of sleep—that the two states are both points on the same awareness continuum—is controversial. Current research suggests that the two states differ biochemically. In other words, a heavily sedated person is not sleeping.

SLEEP APNEA. The inability to breathe and sleep at the same time, resulting in hundreds of momentary brief awakenings to inhale air. People with sleep apnea usually snore at night and may be excessively sleepy during the day.

SLEEP LATENCY. The time between lying down in bed and actually falling asleep.

SOPORIFIC. A general term for a drug capable of diminishing awareness and sometimes able to induce sleep.

STRESS. A challenge to your biological or psychological equilibrium; for example, psychologically to your peace of mind if you experience a loss, or biologically, the inflammatory reaction of skin to poison ivy. The term has come to include also the ways your body systems adapt to a sense of threat or injury.

STIMULANTS. A class of chemicals usually described in terms of effects on the central nervous system. These effects include, for example, more rapid heartbeat and respiratory rate. A euphoria in which everyday inhibitions are suppressed and anxiety is reduced is common with stimulant use. Caffeine is the most widely known and used central nervous system stimulant.

SUBSTANCE. An umbrella term favored in precise medicolegal language to cover a wide variety of ingested material, ranging from prescribed medications to illicit street drugs.

TOLERANCE. Refers to the diminishing effect the original dose of a substance may have; leads to using more and more of this substance to achieve the desired response.

TRANQUILIZER. A general category of drugs primarily intended to promote a sense of ease. Tranquilizers have a calming effect without causing sleep.

AN ANNOTATED GLOSSARY

TRICYCLIC ANTIDEPRESSANTS. A chemical description of a class of drugs, usually used to elevate mood in certain psychologically troubled patients. These drugs have also been used in the treatment of narcolepsy and in the pain/depression/insomnia triad.

WITHDRAWAL. Often refers to the stopping of a patient's medication, to the gradual steps of a treatment plan in which diminishing amounts of a medication are prescribed. Sometimes refers to the appearance of symptoms indicating an adaptation to being without the drug.

HONORABLE MENTIONS

In as new a field as the emerging sleep/wake sciences, a host of pioneers has advanced our knowledge in quantum leaps. Their contribution of bringing this multidisciplinary science into the mainstream of medical practice has helped millions of people with sleep disorders—among them insomnia.

After a thousand and one nights of darkness, sleep mythology has yielded to rational, effective treatment through the efforts of dedicated and imaginative researchers and clinicians. To single out a few from among the many whose insights and writings have illuminated the unexplored continent of insomnia is to salute leadership that made the new sleep/wake sciences possible. Out of a *magna cum laude* roll call of merit numbering in the hundreds, these distinguished scientists deserve *summa cum laude* recognition:

William C. Dement, M.D., Ph.D.
Christian Guilleminault, M.D.
Peter Hauri, Ph.D.
Ernest L. Hartmann, M.D.
Anthony Kales, M.D.

Joyce D. Kales, M.D.
Ismet Karacan, M.D.
Nathaniel Kleitman, Ph.D.
Elliot D. Weitzman, M.D., Ph.D.

AFTERWORD

Inevitably insomnia has become a statistical giant—described in millions of sufferers, millions of dollars, millions of prescriptions, medications, and staggering health care costs.

But the critical number is ONE. YOU.

It's your life, your insomnia, as unique as your fingerprints.

You are the yardstick—how you choose to live, the events in your life, the sleeping pills you may be taking, deserve a day—really a lifetime—of balanced reckoning. The more aware you are of how your waking hours affect your nighttime hours, the less vulnerable you may be to insomnia. You can be informed, and you can make informed choices to help overcome your insomnia. With information and insight you become part of the solution instead of part of the problem.

The pages of this book are reminders that the human condition can be improved, treated, and sometimes cured.

The greatest revolution of our generation is the discovery that human beings, by changing the inner attitudes of their minds, can change the outer aspects of their lives.

William James

INDEX

ABOUT THE AUTHORS

Bernard Dryer is a physician and best-selling novelist. His novels have been published widely around the world in several languages. His medical career includes university faculty appointments in medicine and psychiatry and the directorship of a nationwide study of postgraduate medical education.

Ellen S. Kaplan has had fourteen years' experience in the medical field. Most recently she was a senior medical editor of the American Medical Association's multimedia continuing medical education series.